NO BULL

Object Technology for Executives

Managing Object Technology Series

Additional Volumes in Preparation

NO BULL

Object Technology for Executives

Written and Illustrated by

William S. Perlman

PUBLISHED BY THE PRESS SYNDICATE OF THE UNIVERSITY OF CAMBRIDGE
The Pitt Building, Trumpington Street, Cambridge, United Kingdom

CAMBRIDGE UNIVERSITY PRESS
The Edinburgh Building, Cambridge CB2 2RU, UK
http://www.cup.cam.ac.uk
40 West 20th Street, New York, NY 10011-4211, USA
http://www.cup.org
10 Stamford Road, Oakleigh, Melbourne 3166, Australia

Published in association with SIGS Books

First published in 1999

Design and composition by Susan A. Ahlquist
Cover design by Tom Jezek

Printed in the United States of America

A catalog record for this book is available from the British Library.

Library of Congress Cataloging-in-Publication Data is on record with the publisher.

ISBN 0 521 64548 4 paperback

This book is dedicated to *you*.

(Why not, you paid for it didn't you?)

CONTENTS

ACKNOWLEDGMENTS

I thank The Creator, Jerry and Barbara Perlman (my folks), you, Don Jackson (the guy who was crazy enough to think this book was a good idea), H.R.H. Lothlórien Homet (world-class editor, reviewer, coach, and woman who will move heaven and earth for a bag of peanut M&Ms), and SIGS and Cambridge University Press for the opportunity to create this book. Without all of the preceding, none of the following would have been possible. In addition, I've got to recognize the following people for their HUGE contributions to the overall quality and content of this book:

✪ The great crew at SIGS Publications that made this anti-bovine manifesto look like a *real* book. In particular, thanks to Matt Lusher for beating the lumps out of the manuscript, Tom Jezek for creating a cover that achieved the miracle of looking great and keeping everybody happy, and Susan Ahlquist for making the insides of the book all warm and fuzzy.

✪ Yvonne Perkins, Director, Application Development Technologies, IBM Software Solutions for sharing her candid insights and years of experience both managing software development and producing application development solutions for the world IT community. Her suggestions greatly improved the content of the chapter on managing for object technology.

✪ Laurie Jenson, Manager, Recruitment Services, Customer Information Group, Wells Fargo, for her sage advice, input, and review of the chapter on staffing for object technology.

✪ Brian Starr, former Object-Oriented Solutions Manager, Application Development Technologies, IBM Software Solutions for reviewing the first draft of this manuscript and for his helpful hints.

✪ My folks and Peggy Cole Pate for reviewing the more techie parts of the book and keeping me down to earth. My Dad also deserves credit for giving a little art direction in the nick of time.

Heartfelt appreciation to Arthur Stringer, Boulton Miller, and Titus Purdin for making a difference. Finally, thanks to Doug and Ed (the dog) Ledbetter for donating office space and checking in periodically to make sure I was still breathing during the first draft of this book.

INTRODUCTION

You and I have something in common: We don't have time to waste. You don't have time to read a lot of bull, and I don't have time to write it. This book is for high-level managers and non-technical professionals with little or no computer experience. Its purpose is to give you a direct, easy-to-understand, and practical introduction to *object technology* (OT). It will teach you what OT is, teach you most of the big buzz words, outline the costs and benefits of using OT, and make you aware of the issues involved in staffing and managing for OT.

HOW TO USE THIS BOOK

On your next coast-to-coast redeye, have the flight attendant pour you a double of your favorite beverage, turn on the overhead light (which, of course, will really tick off the guy trying to sleep in the seat next to you), and dig in. You can finish the whole book before the plane even begins its descent. The best part is, by the time you land, you'll know enough to tell that techNOBULLy in your IT department a thing or two about a thing or two. Have at it and have fun! If you have questions or comments about this book, please contact me via the NO BULL home page at the Cambridge University Press Web site at http://www.cup.org/titles/64/0521645484.html.

I EXECUTIVE SUMMARY

MONEY TALKS, AND . . .
(WELL, YOU KNOW)

Object technology is about money—or, more specifically, *profits*. Used intelligently, object technology can result in tremendous reductions in the amount of person-hours required to produce and maintain software systems. That means faster time-to-market, increased competitive advantage, lower software development and maintenance costs, and fewer programmers on the payroll. In short, revenue goes up, cost goes down, customers are happier, and the shareholders get all warm and fuzzy. Used not-so-intelligently, object technology can have very much the opposite effect. This book shows you how to get to the good part without stepping in the bad part.

HOW NOW?
(What is Object Technology?)

This book defines the term *object technology* as tools and techniques for creating software from reusable parts. Object technology is a lot like the idea of interchangeable parts that revolutionized manufacturing. Once an organization has a decent inventory of software *parts*, the parts can be quickly and inexpensively assembled into a wide variety of applications.

SHOOTIN' THE BULL
(Object Terminology)

All the benefits of object technology are made possible through the use of *objects* and *classes*. Classes are the software equivalents of molds used to create mechanical parts. The parts in an *object-oriented* (OO) program are called *objects*. Just like mechanical molds, classes can be reused over and over again to create objects for numerous programs. However, unlike molds for mechanical parts, programmers can also use existing classes to create new classes, or *subclasses*, with additional properties and functionality through a process called *inheritance*. Construction of large, complex object-oriented software systems can be greatly simplified by using *frameworks*, software subassemblies made from reusable parts.

Software architects reduce design time and the risk of bad design by using known design solutions called *patterns*. Object-oriented designs may be expressed through *UML* (*Unified Modeling Language*), a system of diagrams analogous to the blueprints used by structural architects.

WHERE'S THE BEEF?

(WHAT'S IN IT FOR YOU?)

Object technology, when used correctly, enables you to leverage skills across the organization, reduce mid- and long-term software development costs, shorten system development time, and produce higher-quality, more reliable software systems. In short, if you do it right, object technology can help you reduce head count, deploy new and enhanced systems faster, rapidly adapt to market changes, and reduce the number of outages and errors caused by software bugs. Object technology can also be used to facilitate better interoperability with your suppliers' or customers' information systems.

WATCH YOUR STEP
(Now the Bad News)

Contrary to the marketing hype, OT is not a miracle cure and should not be used in all situations. Organizations just venturing into OT for the first time should wade into it cautiously and avoid trying out OT on mission-critical applications. In addition, be prepared to

- ✪ hire new people or contractors because your existing ones may not be up to the challenge.

- ✪ invest in a lot of expensive training for existing software development personnel.

- ✪ pay higher salaries for qualified new hires.

Design expenditures, especially in initial projects, will probably be much higher than in traditional software projects. Because object-oriented software relies heavily on code reuse, poorly designed code not only impacts the cost of the current project, but the cost of future projects as well. In the worst case, a bad design can necessitate a complete rewrite late in a project. Just as a bad mold will make bad mechanical parts, a flawed class will create flawed objects in every program that uses it, and probably every program using its subclasses.

THE ROUND UP
(STAFFING FOR OBJECT TECHNOLOGY)

In staffing for object-oriented software development projects, it is very important to hire developers who have a lot of object-oriented programming experience. This is especially true for the role of system architect. Designers with a lot of traditional programming experience and little or no OT experience can actually destroy an object-oriented project. For junior-level programming positions, it is better to hire someone recently out of school who has been specifically trained in object-oriented languages and techniques.

Beware of so-called *consultant brokers;* they usually do not have the technical savvy to qualify object-oriented architects properly. All consultants should be carefully screened through an interview process with an experienced object-oriented developer. Many programmers who don't have a clue about how to create good object-oriented software can dazzle you with all the object technology buzzwords they read in a book somewhere.

Sometimes it makes more sense to *buy* object technology than build it. Because object-oriented programs are built from reusable components, it's much easier to do this than ever before. If you don't have the skills in-house or can't justify the investment for a certain part of a system, you may be able to purchase the components or subassemblies from outside vendors. This can be dramatically cheaper and faster than building it yourself.

PLOWSHARES AND FERTILIZER
(The Tools of the Trade)

Once you've found the right people to do the job, get the most out of them by putting the right tools in their hands. Object-oriented *CASE* (*Computer Aided Software Engineering*) tools are drafting programs designed to assist software architects in drawing up the plans for object-oriented systems. In addition, many CASE tools can actually use the design drawings to do some of the programming for you.

Perhaps the most important tool decision to make is the choice of what programming language and software development environment to use. Programming languages are as varied as human languages, each with its own strengths and weaknesses. The most popular object-oriented languages are C++, Small-talk, and Java. In addition, *component-based* development systems like Visual Basic, VisualAge, and JavaBeans are very popular for creating software systems from components with minimal programming effort.

Once your company begins to accumulate an inventory of reusable parts, your biggest challenge is software asset management. Since object-oriented components represent a considerable investment in labor and materials, they should be tracked and managed like any other parts inventory. Unless there is an effective system for cataloging, inventorying, and finding the object-oriented components the company has built or purchased, the investment in reusable software is lost.

RIDIN' THE HERD

(MANAGING FOR OBJECT TECHNOLOGY)

No matter how good your team is at developing object-oriented software systems, there is no substitute for competent project management. Object technology by itself will *not make your projects come in on time or under budget*. It's like using a power saw versus a handsaw: Both of them can saw a board or cut off your head, depending on the competence of the user. It's just that the power saw lets you do either one faster.

The first step in making a strategic investment in object technology is having a clear idea of what you want to use it for. The most sure-fire way to do this is to align your investment with the company's goals. The way you invest in object technology for reengineering, for example, is very different than the way you invest in object technology for creating a new line of business.

Probably the most difficult part of introducing object technology into your company will be change management. Introducing new people and new technology is always hard. However, with object technology you're also asking your programmers to change the way they think and unlearn everything they've ever learned about writing software. This is on a par with asking them to adopt a new religion. If the change is not carefully managed, you may encounter fierce resistance, passive or aggressive.

The key to succeeding with object technology is to start small. No matter how good your people are, the first couple of object-oriented projects will probably be a comedy of errors in either design, planning, or execution (and most likely, all of the above). Start with trivial projects. Many companies get themselves in trouble by trying to make some huge, mission-critical thing their first object-oriented development project.

The most challenging aspect of planning for object-oriented software development is estimating. Both because of the iterative way that object-oriented software is built and because of extensive reuse of components, conventional measures of software size often fail to predict the effort within an acceptable range of accuracy. The rule of thumb is: Early object-oriented projects should take longer than traditional projects, and later object-oriented projects should come in a lot faster than traditional projects. The important variable in either case is the level of skill your team has. If your team is new to object technology, the first few projects will take longer and you may not see the return until further down the road than if your team is highly experienced in object technology. Also, the number of components you buy versus the number you build is a key factor in sizing the effort. It also affects how tasks are delegated: Using components from outside vendors may eliminate many tasks that you would have traditionally assigned to a developer.

A final thing to think about when managing for object technology is how to measure success. Keep statistics on productivity, internal and external customer satisfaction, turnaround time, and bugs; compare them against the statistics collected prior to adopting object technology. This information will not only help you determine whether you're getting your money's worth out of object technology, but will also improve the quality of your estimates.

2 HOW NOW?

(What is Object Technology)

"Holy Holsteins, Henrietta! Your people have been working on enhancing that payroll system for two years now. What the !#$^ are you people *doing* down there?!? So far we've dumped $999,999,999,999.99 into that thing, and I still can't even tell what time of day it is! I'm telling you, if that system isn't on-line by the end of the month, you'd better be real *chummy* with your cousin who owns that burger joint . . ."

"Hello Joe? Yeah, hi, it's Bob. You know, your boss . . . yes, it's nice to talk to you, too. Say Joe, I was wondering when you were planning to get that bug out of the production system. Now personally, I don't worry about these things much, but the guys down in accounting tell me these outages are costing us about $1,000,000 per hour and this is the tenth one this week. Do you think perhaps your gang could skip the beer run at lunch today and get this resolved, OR DO I HAVE TO FIRE YOUR @#*!"

Wouldn't it be great to get changes made to your mission critical software in *days* instead of years? Wouldn't it be great if your mission critical applications never had bugs? Yes it would, but we don't have that yet. However, we can get awfully darn close using a thing called *object technology* (OT). OT is an exciting "new" way to rapidly assemble software systems from proven, reusable parts that has actually been around for about thirty years. It evolved from techniques developed for programming simulations and artificial intelligence in the 1960s. These techniques are similar to the way interchangeable parts are used in manufacturing: Software systems are rapidly constructed from a set of common parts. The potential savings in person-hours are enormous.

COMPUTER PROGRAMMING 101

To truly understand what object technology is and what it can do for you, you first need to understand a little bit about the way software was created before the object revolution. Computer programs in their most basic form look a lot like grandma's favorite apple pie recipe: They're made up of ingredients (*data*) and step-by-step instructions (*code*) that tell the computer how to transform the data into a desired form. For example, a *recipe* to calculate the number of miles per gallon your car gets might look something like the following:

RECIPE FOR MILES-PER-GALLON

INGREDIENTS:

✪ Gallons used

✪ Miles traveled

DIRECTIONS:

❶ Enter the number of gallons used.

❷ Enter the number of miles traveled.

❸ Divide the number of miles traveled by the number of gallons used to get miles-per-gallon.[1]

❹ Show the result (miles-per-gallon) to the person using this program

---

[1]Technically, *miles-per-gallon* is also a data item in this program, but since it is the *result* of the program, I left it out of the Ingredients section to avoid confusing things. The Ingredients section really only contains the *inputs* to the program; both final results and intermediate results are also considered data items in real computer programs.

In the programming language *BASIC*, the equivalent computer program might look like this:

```
INPUT "Enter gallons used: ", GallonsUsed
INPUT "Enter miles traveled: ", MilesTraveled
MilesPerGallon = MilesTraveled / GallonsUsed
PRINT "Your Gas Mileage = "; MilesPerGallon
```

For simple applications like the gas mileage program, this style of programming is very effective. Unfortunately, programs in today's world are seldom this short. For instance, your favorite word processing program may have over a hundred thousand data items and more than a million instructions. While large programs present no special problem for the computer, they're a nightmare for the humans who have to improve and maintain them. Software created in this *unstructured* manner rapidly becomes far too complex for any one human to understand. As a result, the larger an unstructured program becomes, the harder it is for a single programmer to make changes to it without inadvertently introducing bugs.

Imagine Grandma trying to shop for over a hundred thousand ingredients without forgetting anything on the list; imagine Grandma trying to keep her place in an apple pie recipe with over a million steps (many of which refer back to other steps); imagine Grandma laughing hysterically as the men in little white suits carry her away. Needless to say, programmers found a more manageable way to create software.

THE VILLAGE SMITTY

Computer programs are very much custom products. A given program may be *copied* millions of times on diskettes, but the program itself is only created once. For this reason the software development process closely resembles a *job shop*. A job shop is a manufacturing operation that makes small-production-run, custom products like commercial airplanes and leather saddles. It is therefore not surprising that the evolution of software engineering practices closely parallels the evolution of manufacturing engineering. Sadly, the software community is about fifty to seventy-five years behind manufacturing on the learning curve. In fact, it's very likely the software group in your company still uses programming techniques on a technological par with the village blacksmith. (Hmmm . . . maybe *that's* why you smell manure every time they tell you why a project is overdue and over budget.)

In the early job shops, a handful of skilled craftspeople performed all aspects of production. Jobs were handled one at a time, one or two craftspeople worked on each job, and everything was built from the ground up. Believe it or not, this is exactly the way a great deal of software is still built: A handful of programmers work together to create most or all of a given program from scratch—every time! As a result, software development organizations are plagued by the same problems that afflicted the early job shops: duplication of effort, interfering work, hard-to-replace workers, eternal production cycles, and

late delivery. In addition, this style of development usually results in the construction of poorly structured software. As shown in the previous section, the confusion caused by this type of coding greatly increases the probability of *bugs* (programmer errors) as the size of your software system grows.

The first major advance in job shop technology was the introduction of *specialization of labor*, the movement that defined the twentieth-century factory. Its central principle is that the production of a given product should be broken down into a series of discrete steps, each performed by a specialist who performs *only* that kind of task. Breaking the process up like this makes it easier to plan and manage the flow of materials, reduces the skill set required for any given worker, and allows work to be done in parallel. It also minimizes duplication of effort and instances of one worker interfering with another.

Perhaps the most dramatic effect of specialization of labor was the way it changed product design. No longer did product designers have the luxury of thinking of a product as some big blob that needed to be built. Instead, the designer had to become aware of all functional aspects of the product, breaking it up into the machining operations required to manufacture it. If it needed a ½" hole, it went to the drill press; if it needed one surface polished, it went to the polishing and grinding station; and so on. In this way, not only was it possible to efficiently route any given product through the system, but manufacturers could *reuse* common machine set-ups for many different products. For example, if widget x and widget y both need ½" holes,

they can both be routed to the drill press while it is set up for
½″ holes. It wasn't until more than half a century later that this
way of thinking was introduced into the software community.

In the late 1960s a software development movement called
structured programming evolved. Unlike unstructured programs, which are basically one big glob of instructions and
data, structured programs are a collection of relatively small,
independent units called *modules*. Each module contains a
small group of instructions and data, and performs a specific
function in the software system. For example, a checkbook

program may be divided into one module that handles transactions, another module that prints checks, and still another module that performs reconciliations. If any one module becomes too big, it too can be subdivided into functional units called *functions* or *procedures*. Continuing with the checkbook program example, the module that handles transactions could be broken down into two procedures: one to debit the account and one to credit the account. Functions and procedures themselves can also be subdivided if necessary. There are several advantages to developing software in a structured way:

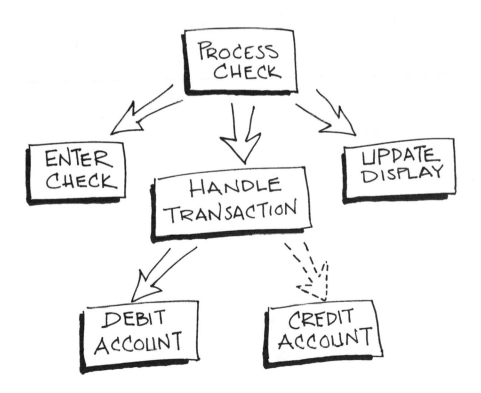

✪ **Programs that are broken down into small, specialized chunks are easier to understand, add to, and debug.** Even Granny picked up on this idea. You will often see a pie recipe broken up into procedures for making the crust, making the filling, making the topping, and so on. This is much easier than trying to follow a recipe that has instructions for all of the above lumped together. In software development, the net result is that it is far easier to train new people, and fewer bodies are required to maintain and develop code.

✪ **Procedures written for one program can be reused in other programs.** This means new programs can be created faster and with less labor. For example, the same debit-account routine from the checkbook program could also be used to debit an asset account in a general ledger program. This is analogous to a certain die being used in the manufacture of both widget x and widget y—we only have to create and set up the die once to make both products.

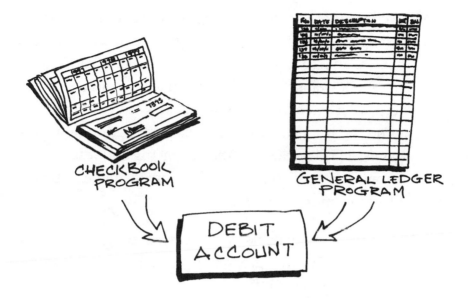

❂ **Structured programming makes it easier to develop software in teams.** Individuals can be assigned specific modules to program, which enables them to work concurrently with other developers. Think of the pie recipe. In order to get the pie into the oven faster, one person could make the crust, while another made the filling. In addition, the development of modules, functions, or procedures can be assigned to individuals based on their area of expertise. For example, a function to do financial forecasting could be written by a programmer with a background in statistics, while a procedure to display a graph could be written by a programmer with experience in graphics programming. This is directly akin to the specialization of labor in manufacturing.

✪ *Well written* **structured programs are more resistant to bugs.** Just as workers in well-defined functional areas are less able to interfere with one another's work, functions in a well structured program are less able to interfere with each other's data. Also, modules proven error-free in one application can be reused in new programs. This leverages all the debugging and testing performed on the original application to make the new programs more reliable.

Despite the obvious benefits of structured programming, it wasn't until the 1970s that programmers really began to accept it. However, even today huge amounts of code are still written in an unstructured fashion. What this costs the global economy is incalculable. Imagine a world in which job shops still operated as they did before the industrial revolution. This is the state of *modern* software development.

CLOSE, BUT NO CIGAR

By now you're probably thinking, "Hey, this structured programming stuff sounds like the best thing since bell-bottom
jeans and polyester suits! I'm going to rush right out of here
and call a meeting to form a committee to draft a memo to my
IT managers to tell all their people to be sure their people are
using this stuff!" *Not so fast!* We can do better. Structured programming is a vast improvement over unstructured programs,
but it's far from perfect.

Structured programming does extremely well for small- to
medium-size software systems. However, in very large systems,
it begins to fail us. A large program may be made up of hundreds of modules, each using dozens of procedures and functions. While structured programs *are* far easier to understand
and modify than unstructured programs, large ones often go
beyond the reach of human comprehension. When this is the
case, development and service times tend to develop stretch
marks. The more complex the program, the less likely it is that
any one programmer fully understands it. As a result, most programmers on large, established projects spend the majority of
their time trying to understand code rather than writing it. This
is why enhancements to mission critical systems often end up
late and over budget.

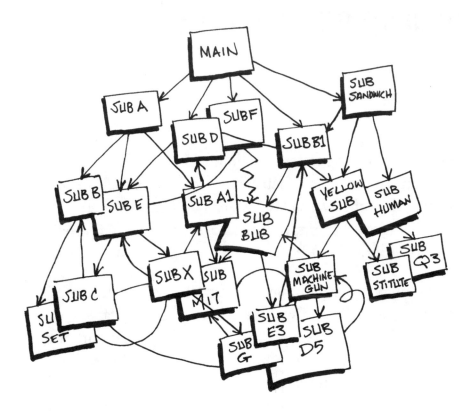

Another unpleasant side effect of high software complexity is the proliferation of bugs. Most of these result from code modifications made by programmers who did not fully understand the implications of their changes. Because understanding all the effects of a change in a large system is virtually impossible, programmers are often forced to just make an educated guess. The quality of this guess is directly related the amount of experience the programmer has with the particular software system in question. However, even programmers with decades of experience frequently guess wrong. The resulting bugs are usually insidious and may take weeks or even months to fix.

Perhaps the ultimate casualty of software size is code reuse. Many executives define code reuse as reusing legacy code from release to release of a software system. This *is* code reuse, but it's not the kind that holds the most potential to save you money and is not what programmers mean when they say *code reuse*. Reuse, as programmers refer to it, is the ability to write a block of code only once, yet be able to use its functionality in different areas of the same program or in an entirely different program. Recall the way the debit account routine from the checkbook program was reused in a general ledger application in the previous section. The more you can do this, the less person-hours are required to produce software—it also reduces the likelihood of bugs. The reason is the same as why printing a hundred wedding invitations takes much less time and is less prone to mistakes than writing each one by hand. Unfortunately, reuse in structured programs gets harder to manage as software size grows.

In large software systems it's often hard for programmers to know what code can be reused. For example, suppose a programmer working on a large, sophisticated financial application needs a routine that updates an account balance. In a financial application it is very likely that such a procedure already exists. The programmer, however, may end up writing the procedure from scratch not knowing that another programmer already created it for use somewhere else. It's not that the programmer is incompetent, it's just that in a program containing thousands of procedures, it's impossible to know them all. This problem is so serious that often programmers working in offices right next to each other end up spending days writing exactly the same code! How much does *that* cost the company? It's like the old saying, "When two people in business agree, one of them isn't necessary."

OBJECT TECHNOLOGY TO THE RESCUE

Around the same time structured programming came into existence, researchers in engineering simulations and artificial intelligence were cooking up a style of programming of their own. Since both of these kinds of software systems are designed to model things, the things that happen to things, and the things that things do, it only made sense to program based on things (objects) rather than functions. Little did they know that what they had really done was to lay the foundation for programming techniques that would revolutionize how *all* software is made. However, once again if the software people had taken a cue from manufacturing they would have seen it coming a mile away.

The manufacturing equivalent of object technology is the concept of interchangeable parts. Interchangeable parts are parts designed in such a way that they can be used as components of numerous different products. The advantage of this approach is that a variety of customized products can be rapidly assembled from off-the-shelf components. These components can either be produced in-house or purchased from outside vendors. Not only does this improve the speed of production, but it also allows design and tooling costs to be distributed over more products, reduces the amount of product-specific custom work that needs to be done, and reduces the defect rate. In addition, thinking of products in terms of parts and subassemblies helps product engineers in designing complex systems. These are exactly the reasons to use *object-oriented* programming.

The key advantages of object-oriented programming over structured programming are:

❶ **Object-orientation makes it easier to reuse code.** In structured programming, code reuse usually involves a manual process of cutting and pasting code from one application to another, then customizing it to work in the new program. Object-oriented programming languages inherently support code reuse. Just as plastic parts can be formed from high-speed injection molding, software "molds," called classes, are used to instantly crank out the parts (objects) of an object-oriented program. A given class can be used to create as many parts as needed for *any* program that needs parts of that type. Classes can also be used to create new classes with more features. This would be like being able to make better mechanical molds using the ones you already have.

❷ **Object-oriented software can be created much faster.** Even though structured programs allow a limited amount of code reuse, almost all aspects of them have to be custom-built. Object-oriented programs are, on the other hand, primarily constructed from standardized parts. These parts are created from stock classes, which are either developed in-house or purchased from outside vendors. Just as in the design and creation of mechanical molds, the design and creation of classes can be *very* time consuming. However, once an organization has developed or purchased a decent *class library,* programmers can rapidly assemble new applications from the parts those classes produce. For example, a stock class called **Account** could be used to produce a part called **checkingAccount** in a checkbook program, and a part called **assetAccount** in a general ledger program.

❸ **Object-oriented programs provide better protection against bugs than structured ones.** Object-oriented programs help reduce the likelihood of bugs for all the same reasons that structured programs do. In addition, object-oriented programming languages have features that allow an object's internal data and workings to be sealed off so they cannot be affected by other objects— this is what the propellerheads call *encapsulation.* Inadvertent modification of data is one of the most common and harmful kinds of bugs. Encapsulation also helps reduce software defects by allowing changes to be made to the internals of an object without affecting the code that uses the object.

❹ **Large object-oriented programs are easier for programmers to understand.** Reading a large structured program can get confusing because it's basically nothing more than a collection of hundreds or even thousands of little tasks. After a while that gets to be like a nagging spouse: honey, balance the checkbook; honey, print the report; honey, debit the account; honey, do this, honey do that, and so on. It gets so overwhelming you just start to forget, tune it out, or simply get lost. In a household, that usually results in a fight; in software, that usually results in a bug. Object-oriented programs, as the name implies, are centered around *things* not *tasks*. It is far less confusing to think about a program as a system composed of interconnected parts and subassemblies than as a great big to-do list, structured or not.

Survival in business depends on the ability to adapt quickly to changes: competitive, technological, regulatory, societal, and economic. Since the core of most businesses today is their information systems, it stands to reason that these systems must be highly adaptable as well. The answer is object technology. It enables mission-critical systems to be modified faster and with less risk, and it allows new systems to be rapidly assembled from proven, off-the-shelf components.

3 SHOOTIN' THE BULL
(OBJECT TERMINOLOGY)

Without question, the hardest part about understanding object technology is understanding all the jargon. To laypeople and even to many programmers, *object-speak* sounds like the ramblings of a Zen master in the late stages of senile dementia. Take, for example, this quotation from *Smalltalk and Object Orientation: An Introduction* (Hunt, 1997): "[Polymorphism] is the ability to send the same message to different instances which may appear to perform the same function. However, the way in which the message is handled will depend on the class of which the instance is an example." What?!? The really scary part is that by the time you finish this chapter, you should know enough terminology to understand the preceding sentence (although I'm still struggling with it myself).

If you want to make competent software investment decisions, it is critical that you understand and converse in object-speak; you can't necessarily count on your usual technical advisors. MIS and software professionals commonly learn to ape the words without really understanding their meaning or implications just so they seem up with the times. Even some top-ranked consultants claiming to be experts on the subject are winging it. As a result, many executives have been song-and-danced into huge losses. This chapter will not make you an expert on the subject, but it will teach you enough to follow a conversation about object-oriented software and will give you the tools to smell a rat. More importantly, think of the hit you'll be at cocktail parties: "Hurry *up* Skippy . . . Jim's talking about those objective oriental things again! . . . and get that *@#! *lampshade* off your head!"

WHAT ARE OBJECTS?

Computer programs, especially in business, are systems that model real-world things and events. For example, a point-of-sale system is just a computer program that does exactly what a human does with a cigar box, a notepad, and a stock ledger. An inventory program maintains information about the physical items in inventory, just like the old guy with the visor and the clipboard did. As the name implies, object technology centers around software entities called *objects*. Objects are building blocks (parts) from which programmers can assemble computer programs.

An object in a computer program is nothing more than a glob of computer memory that contains information about a specific thing, like the customer Bob Smith. How that information is formatted and how the object can manipulate it is determined by the object's *class*. A class is the way programmers express the design of an object. The class is the cookie cutter, the object is the cookie, and the computer's memory is the dough; or if you prefer, the class is the mold, the object is the part, and the computer's memory is the molten metal. However, for now, just picture objects as being components that can be stuck together to build complete, custom software systems.

Building software from objects is very much like building physical devices from interchangeable parts. Just as a single type of component can be used to create numerous different kinds of machines, a given type of object can be used to create many different software systems. The type of small speaker used in your television set could also be used in a portable radio or a talking alarm clock. The type of **Account** object used to manage a particular customer's **creditAccount** in a receivables program can also be used to represent a specific **vendorAccount** in a payables program; the same type of **Horn** that adorns your favorite bull's head (**bullHorn**), could also be a **vikingHelmetHorn** or an **texasHoodOrnamentHorn**.

By the way, in case you're wondering why I keep smashing some words together, it's not a typo—this is just a little notation thing: Class names in this book will be one or more words scrunched together, in bold, with each word capitalized; object names will be one or more words scrunched together, in bold and underlined, with the first word in lowercase and all following words (if there are any) in uppercase. Object *attributes* (more on that later) will either follow the object naming rules: an object can be an attribute of another object (for example, an **eyeBall** is an object that is an attribute of a **bookReader** object)—or if the attribute is *not* an object (for example, **heightInInches**) then the same rules apply except there is no underline. Yes this is a goofy way to do it, but it's a common way that programmers represent objects and classes in computer programs. You'll really wow those programmers if your memos use this kind of notation!

When a new object is created from a given class, it is said to be *instantiated*. The **customer**, Bob Smith, is an *instance* (an object) of the class of things called **Customer**. Object-oriented programmers often substitute the word *instance* for the word *object*.

WHAT ARE CLASSES?

Each object in an object-oriented program represents some *thing* like a customer, an employee, an inventory item, a window on the screen, or even an entity that only exists in the programmer's imagination. How a given object in the computer's memory represents its corresponding thing is determined by the object's *class*. Classes specify the *relevant* features (*attributes* and *behaviors*) that an object in a particular program must possess in order to represent a thing. A class is an *abstraction*.

BULL   COOKIE-CUTTER   COOKIE

The thing-class-object relationship is like the relationship between a bull, a bull-shaped cookie cutter (an abstraction of the bull), and a bull-shaped cookie (a particular instance of that abstraction). The cookie cutter represents just enough of the bull's characteristics to produce cookies that *look* like a bull without exactly replicating a bull. (Let's face it, cookies that stink, weigh over 2,000 pounds, and leave manure everywhere probably won't go over too well with company.) More importantly, that level of detail just isn't necessary to make a cookie that represents a bull. The same is true in object-oriented software. Let's use a telemarketing program as an example.

Four key elements in a telemarketing system are: the operators who make the calls and take the orders, the customers who place orders or refuse to buy, the orders themselves, and the products that the customers order. The programmer of this type of system might therefore create four classes of objects: **Operator**, **Customer**, **Order**, and **Product**. For example, the programmer might design a **Customer** class, which produces objects with the attributes **name**, **address**, **phoneNumber**, **customerNumber**, and **creditCardNumber** and the *behaviors* **placeOrder()**, **cancelOrder()**, and **rejectSale().** (Notice that behavior names are differentiated from attribute names by putting empty parentheses "()" at the end of the name—again, it's a programmer thing.) These are the attributes and behaviors *necessary* to represent customers in this program. The programmer probably would *not*, however, include the attribute **noseHairLength** or the behavior **scratchHead()** because (most likely) they have no relevance in a telemarketing system. The Customer class is an *abstract* representation—it produces customer objects that only have the characteristics *required for this application*, not all the possible characteristics of a real customer.

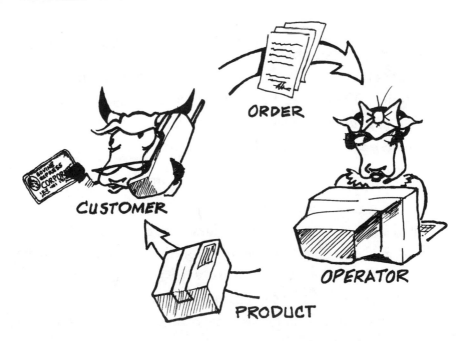

ORDER

CUSTOMER

OPERATOR

PRODUCT

The use of classes to express abstract representations of things is how object-oriented programming helps reduce confusion in large, complex software systems. It is much easier for a programmer to think about all the things *in* a telemarketing system and what they do than to try to remember all the functions that need to be performed *by* a telemarketing system. Also, when the innards of a program are easy to understand, it is more likely that the externals (the parts users see) will be easy to understand. Object-oriented programming forces programmers to do something they don't normally do: think about the *real* world.

ATTRIBUTES AND BEHAVIORS

The *attributes* of an object are simply data items stored in the computer's memory, like the name of a person or the balance of an account. These data items, often called *instance variables, member data, data members,* or just *members* (these terms are all synonyms), are usually hidden within the object.

It's very important to understand the difference between an *instance* of a class and that instance's attribute values. In object-oriented software, as in life, *the values of an object's attributes are not what make an object unique.* For example, imagine you have a friend named Mary Q. Contrary who goes into the witness protection program. She can change her name, her Social Security number, and her hair color; she can get plastic surgery and move to another state; even her recorded birth date may be different. Nonetheless, she's still the same person—even if he/she changes gender—she's still the same person because she still exists. The same is true in software.

Suppose a class called **Customer** is used to create a **creditCardCustomer** object for each credit card customer stored in a banking program. When a teller requests information for a particular customer, the **name** attribute of each **creditCardCustomer** object is queried to produce a list for the teller to select from. Suppose two of the customer names in the system are Bertha Jones and Bertha Smith: each person is represented as a unique **creditCardCustomer** object in the computer's memory. What happens if Betha Jones decides she wants a more exotic name and changes her last name to Smith? The value of the **name** attribute for the **creditCardCustomer** object that represents her changes to "Bertha Smith"; no new object was created in the system, only the name attribute changed in the existing object. The result is that now there are two *unique* **creditCardCustomer** objects in the system that have the **name** value "Bertha Smith."

Normally, the only way to access or change an object's data members is through some behavior of the object. This is quite natural if you think about how things work in the real world. No one knows your name unless you or someone else tells them. No one else can change your address—your address only changes if you move. The ability to move or tell someone your name are your behaviors. This way of looking at data is a big change from structured programming.

The *behaviors* of an object, also called *member functions* or *methods,* are really nothing more than small blocks of computer instructions that perform some operation on member data. Actually, there are two types of member functions: the kind that anybody can use, and the kind that only the object can use internally. The ones anybody can use are called the *behaviors* or *interface* of the object. The internal ones are simply procedures the object uses to get its work done. In fact, an object's *methods* are virtually equivalent to a structured program's *procedures.* However, the *role* an object's methods play in an object-oriented software system is very different from the role procedures play in structured programs.

In a structured program everything is organized around functions (procedures) and functions within functions. Specific items of data flow loosely through one function and on to the next. The programmer must know everything about all the data items used in a procedure and all the subprocedures used by the procedure. In an object-oriented program the programmer only needs to know about the behaviors of an object; the data members and internal procedures of the object are hidden. In other words, you don't have to know the physics of how a telephone works to call your grandmother, and you don't have to know anything about neuroanatomy to ask her how to make an apple pie. This is called *data-hiding* or *encapsulation.*

The way objects in an object-oriented program are wired together is through their behaviors. An object causes another object to do something by sending the other object a *message.* Sending a message to an object causes it to perform a specific behavior. In other words, if you yank the cat's tail, she meows. When you press the on-button on the TV set, you send a message to the TV to turn on—you invoke its **turnOn()** method.

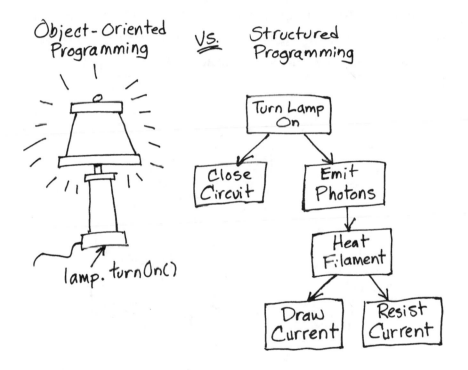

ENCAPSULATION

More than any other single aspect of object technology, the *encapsulation* provided by objects gives us the greatest return on investment. To fully understand the benefits of encapsulation, think of those automated photobooths they have at county fairs. You put money in, you and your friends scramble into the booth, you make goofy faces, the flashbulb goes off a few times, then a few minutes later the pictures come out of the slot. When you put your money into a photobooth, you, in effect, pass the machine a *take-picture* message. In response, it starts its **takePicture()** procedure: it uses its *internal* materials and processes to give you what you want—pictures. You can't see or interfere with what it does to produce the pictures— it's *hidden* from you, and that's exactly what encapsulation is all about.

Hiding the internal workings of the photobooth is a really good idea for several reasons. First, it greatly simplifies things: you don't need to know anything about cameras, film, or photo-processing to get your picture taken. All you have to know is how to put money in the slot. Encapsulation reduces complexity for the object-oriented programmer in a similar fashion. Rather than having to know *everything* about an area of a software system, a programmer only needs to know just enough to use an object to get a desired result.

Another advantage to hiding the internal workings of the photobooth is that it protects them from *you*. Big klutz that you are, if you had access to the guts of the thing you'd probably expose the film to light or knock over a tray of chemicals or something. Similarly, *information hiding* protects member data from being trampled on by klutzy programmers. By far, the vast majority of all software defects come from programmers who write routines that squash the living daylights out of some other programmer's data. If you'll pardon the pun, a programmer in non–object-oriented software is like a *bull* in a china shop. Encapsulation puts data out of harm's way—you can't squash it if you can't get to it.

The final benefit of encapsulating the workings of the photobooth are that the owner can change them at any time without affecting the users. Imagine the owner decides to switch from mechanical to digital photography equipment. This means a great cost savings and you get better quality pictures, faster. Does this mean you now have to learn anything about digital photography to use the photobooth? Of course not! You still do things the way you always did. You put the money in, pose, then wait for your pictures. Likewise, encapsulation of objects reduces the impact of code changes. As long as the external *interface*, the behaviors, of a class of objects remains unchanged, you can change the internal workings freely. This means you can get new functionality faster with fewer bugs.

Sometimes programmers will defeat encapsulation in the name of performance. Don't buy this—it's usually poor design or laziness that's the real motivation. Object-oriented code with poor encapsulation of objects can be worse than unstructured code. The less protection (encapsulation) data has, the higher the probability of bugs.

INHERITANCE

Want to reduce the number of person-hours required to produce software? Reuse code as much as possible. Object-oriented programming languages facilitate code reuse in two ways. The primary way is the ability to crank out an unlimited number of objects from a given class. The other way is called *inheritance*. Inheritance is a feature of object-oriented programming languages that allows all of the attributes and behaviors of one class, called the *base class* or *parent class*, to be used as the foundation for other classes, called *subclasses* or *child classes*. This is like having mechanical molds that not only can be used to create parts, but new molds as well. In addition to the attributes and behaviors inherited from the parent class, a child class may have attributes and behaviors of its own.

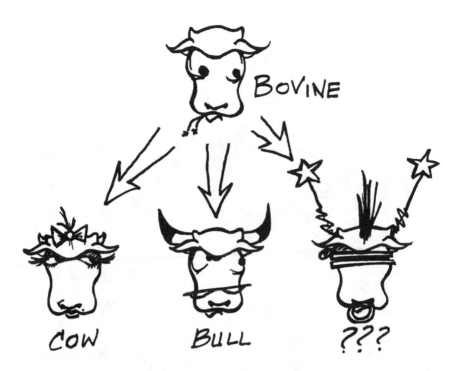

Continuing with the example of the **Customer** class, this class could be used to create an new subclass called **PreferredCustomer**. The **PreferredCustomer** class would contain all of the attributes, like **name**, **address**, **phoneNumber**, etc., and all the behaviors, such as **placeOrder()**, **cancelOrder()**, from the **Customer** class. However, in addition, the programmer could extend it to add a new attribute, **creditLimit**, and a new behavior, **chargeToAccount()**. The key is that this is *all* the programmer has to do; everything else comes from the **Customer** class. The ability to inherit code from an ancestry of classes allows programmers to extend existing applications or to build entirely new ones rapidly.

In addition to extending the base class features, an inherited class can also override or modify inherited behaviors. For example, the **placeOrder()** behavior of the **Customer** class could be overridden by the **PreferredCustomer** class so that when a **preferredCustomer** object places an order, that customer gets a special discount. The amazing part is that *no other changes to the program are required*—the **placeOrder()** behavior of a **preferredCustomer** object is requested by other objects in the system exactly the same way it is for any other **customer** object. We see this in nature all the time. The **Bull**, **Chicken**, and **Human** classes of things all inherit from the class of things called **Animals**. All **Animals eat()**. However, *how* we all **eat()** is very different, and is determined by what **Animal** *subclass* we belong to. This is what programmer types call *polymorphism*— behaviors common to a general class of things being performed differently depending on what subclass a particular thing belongs to. Eating is a *polymorphic* **Animal** behavior. Object-oriented programming languages that support polymorphism enable programmers to create more flexible software systems. New types of objects can easily be introduced into existing software without having to change any code.

Another strange little feature of some object-oriented programming languages is *multiple inheritance*. Multiple inheritance simply means that a given subclass inherits from more than one parent class. In other words, baby has Daddy's eyes and Mommy's nose. In practice, this type of inheritance is not widely used because it can create some *very* ugly situations. For example, if you have one class called **RevolvingAccount** and another called **MortgageLoan**, and for some reason you want to offer a mortgage that charges interest like a revolving account, you could use them to create a new class called **RevolvingMortgage**. Now suppose both parent classes have a behavior called **makePayment()**—which version will **RevolvingMortgage** use? The answer is: Who knows? This type of problem is exactly why most object-oriented languages do not support multiple inheritance. In all but the exceptional cases, your programmers should refrain from using it.

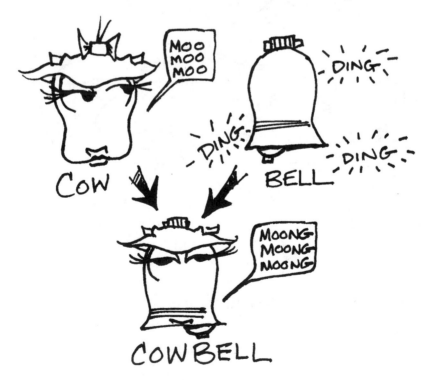

FRAMEWORKS

In very large, complex software systems, the number of objects involved can become unmanageable. Just as an executive in a large company would have trouble directly managing a team of ten thousand employees, programmers have trouble managing object-oriented software systems that have hundreds or even thousands of objects. The solution for the executive is to divide the company into divisions, organizations, and departments; the solution for the software architect is to organize classes in an object-oriented program by logical groupings of objects called frameworks.

Each framework can be thought of as a kind of gigantic class, and each usage (or *instance*) of that framework can be thought of as a monster object with its own special characteristics. For example, most PC programs these days have a *graphical user interface (GUI)*. A software tools vendor could build a GUI framework that was made up of hundreds of classes of user interface objects, like **buttons**, **menus**, **cursors**, **scrollBars**, etc. The same GUI framework may be purchased and used to build the GUI for a company developing a word processing program and a company developing a spreadsheet program. Each program uses an instance of the GUI framework, but the *way* each program uses *and extends* it is very different. A car manufacturer can use the same engine in a sedan and a pickup truck, but the gearing, type of transmission, suspension, frame, and chassis attached to it are very different. As a result the functional and operational characteristics of the two vehicles are very different.

While we're on the subject of cars, another way to think about frameworks is to equate them to prefabricated subassemblies in manufacturing. For example, a car can be decomposed into the engine subassembly, the chassis subassembly, the transmission subassembly, and so on. The company may make its own chassis and engine, but buy the transmission from an overseas manufacturer. A video game could be divided into a user interface framework and a game-rules framework. The video game company would probably write the game logic, but they might buy the framework for creating the user interface from somebody else. Why go to all the trouble and expense to invent something yourself that somebody else is mass producing and selling cheap?

PATTERNS

So far in this chapter we have just talked about the raw materials from which object-oriented programs are built. Just as boards and nails don't form themselves into a house, the components of an object-oriented program don't just randomly assemble themselves into a software system. Behind every system is one or more architects or designers who select, structure, and arrange the elements that will comprise the system.

The tasks performed by a software architect are not entirely different from those performed by a structural architect. Both strive to create an elegant design that fills the functional need of the customer. Their work begins with thorough research into the requirements of the customer and the problem space in which they are to create. For the structural architect, the problem space is defined by the site characteristics and its surroundings and the functional needs of the customer; for the software architect, the problem space is defined by the existing hardware, software, the organizational structure, and the type of work the software system is to perform. Are we building a house, a church, or a skyscraper? Are we building an integrated manufacturing system, a spacecraft control system, or a video game? The desert or the city? A twenty-two-million-dollar supercomputer or a twenty-two-hundred-dollar PC?

As with everything else, computer scientists are way behind most other disciplines, in their analysis and design techniques. In fact, the most earth-shattering advance in software design of the 1990s, *patterns*, was borrowed directly from a 1977 architecture text: *A Pattern Language: Towns, Buildings, Construction* by Christopher Alexander, Sara Ishikawa, and Murray Silverstein. Alexander and the gang advanced a very simple theory: in the design of *anything* (not just towns, buildings, and construction, as the title suggests), there are certain basic problems that keep popping up over and over again. A system of patterns identifies, names, and catalogs common design problems and their proven (by research and experience) fundamental solutions. Patterns allow architects to reuse design solutions just like classes allow programmers to reuse code, and the benefits are the same: faster completion of task, fewer mistakes.

A pattern has four key elements[1]:

❶ a name by which it can be referenced

❷ a description of a *general* problem and the situation in which it occurs

❸ a generalized solution

❹ the trade-offs of implementing the solution.

Using patterns gives designers a higher level way to describe a common situation. Instead of having to describe the problem to be solved in detail, the designer can reference the situation by its pattern name. For instance, you find yourself owning a farm and suddenly realize you need a place to confine your prize bull overnight to keep him from helping your cows make prize calves while you sleep. So, being the progressive, object-oriented farmer that you are, you quickly pull out your book of farm design patterns, and look for a solution to the problem. After a quick search, you find a patterned called a "Stall." Here's what it says:

<u>Pattern</u>: STALL

<u>Problem</u>: Need to isolate and contain a large animal for a limited period of time.

---

[1] This information is roughly paraphrased from *Design Patterns: Elements of Reusable Object-Oriented Software*, Erich Gamma et al., (Addison-Wesley Publishing Company, Inc., 1995).

Context: It is often necessary to keep a large animal in small space to keep it calm and to keep it from doing harm or other mischief to your property or other animals. Some important uses include feeding (to avoid being trampled in a stampede for the hay), grooming and cleaning, and preventing unauthorized nocturnal procreation of the species.

Solution: A small, three sided room, with walls constructed of a material heavy enough to withstand high impact kicks and charges from large animals. The fourth side of the room should be a gate of some kind that is wide enough to allow a very large animal to enter and exit easily. The gate should also be made of a very sturdy material and have a latching mechanism and hinges strong enough to resist repeated kicks and charges by a very large, powerful animal. Be sure that not only are the hinges strong, but the material securing them to the wall is strong as well. The space should be large enough that the animal can turn around, but small enough to limit fully extended kicks to the surrounding walls. Also, the floor should be covered with a replaceable material that is capable of absorbing moisture, odors, spilled food, and waste products. The structure should also have a roof and be fully enclosed to minimize exposure to the elements.

Trade-offs:

- ✪ The animal might be a little testy or, conversely, lethargic when it is released.

✪ Construction of a STALL requires a great deal more effort than simply tying the animal to a tree or a post. However, the STALL is much more secure.

Notice that the description of a pattern *includes no real specifics about* implementation. For example, based on the pattern above, a STALL could be made out of brick with a lovely French wrought iron gate and hardwood floors covered with kitty litter. There is also nothing that says you can't put in air-conditioning and a stereo. This pattern could be just as easily adapted to an elephant as a bull or a sheep. *There is nothing that makes the solution specific to cattle.* The description above doesn't even suggest that the stall has to be inside a barn—it could be its own free-standing structure. Of course, the more standard implementation *is* inside a barn and is a wooden structure with a gate made out of hollow metal tubing and dirt floors covered with sawdust. A final key point is that little details we take for granted are included in the solution, e.g., hinges securely fastened to the wall. Some poor farmer way back in history had to find out that his nice big strong stall, with its big strong gate, didn't hold his prize bull in because the nails in the hinges were too small to hold a charging bull.

The main advantage of using patterns is that they keep you from reinventing the wheel every time you design something. Also, pattern names give object-oriented architects a convenient language with which to discuss design situations in a high-level way, rather than getting into the specifics of the problem. Which is easier to talk about, building a *stall* or building a "small structure for overnight containment of a bull that's easy to lead him into and out of that he can't kick down or escape from so he won't get into trouble or aggravate the cows or something while you sleep"?

The danger with patterns is they can foster laziness. It is always easier to reach into your bag of known tricks and pull out a quick fix than to spend a little time, think through a problem, and come up with an innovative (and, hopefully, better) solution. Where else will new patterns come from? Even though a generic solution to a problem may work in a given situation, other factors may make some other solution better suited to the purpose. Nonetheless, if nothing else, a pattern can serve as a good starting point.

UNIFIED MODELING LANGUAGE (UML)

Once architects start to understand the problem space, ideas begin to flow. The first step may be a few rough sketches of a general shape on the back of a napkin. These initial sketches are bounced around with the team and the customer, and eventually, they evolve into incredibly detailed, complex drawings that leave nothing to the imagination. As implementation progresses the picture may change: Some ideas just don't work, the customer changes her mind, the problem definition changes a little, politics, etc.

A graphical plan of the thing to be built not only allows designers to understand and refine their concepts, but facilitates communication of ideas to others as well. However, the only way this communication can effectively take place is if all parties involved speak the same *graphical language*—i.e., the symbols used in the drawing mean the same thing to the designer, the customer, and the builders.

The graphical language of the structural architect includes the types of drawings (floor plans, elevations, etc.) and symbols (door sweeps, windows, etc.) used in blueprints. The graphical language of the software architect is the Unified Modeling Language. However, unlike the parts of buildings, which pretty much stay put (unless there's an earthquake or a flood or something), the components of software systems are in constant motion. A user pushes a button on a user interface, some data gets retrieved, some other object gets created, it sends a signal to a third object, a fourth object gets deleted, and the dance continues. . . . As a result, UML contains many more types of diagrams and symbols than are found in architectural blueprints.

UML defines nine different kinds of diagrams. Simplified samples of each type are shown below:[2]

---

[2]The following information was loosely extracted from Muller, Pierre-Alain, *Instant UML*, by Pierre-Alain Muller (Wrox Press Ltd., 1997).

❶ **Use Case Diagram**—critical to the analysis phase of a project. Use cases attempt to identify the functional needs of the user. This diagram shows the *actors* in a system and represents the things they do within the boundaries of the system and the things the system does for them. An actor may be an end user, an administrator, hardware connected to the system, or other systems.

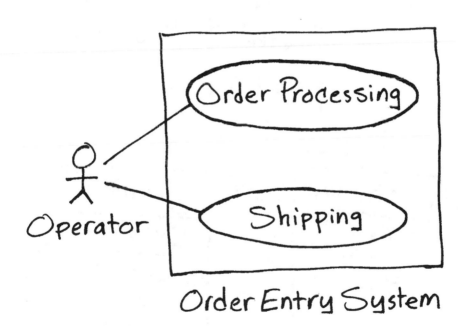

Order Entry System

❷ **Class Diagram**—shows the general structure of an object-oriented program and relationships between the classes that comprise it. Classes are represented as three-tiered rectangles: the top tier is the class name, the middle tier is a list of all the attributes of the class, and the bottom tier is a list of all the class' methods.

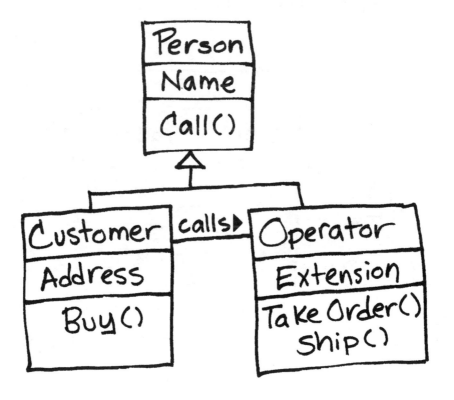

❸ **Object Diagram**—(also called an *instance diagram*) represents objects and the connections between them. Each object is represented by a rectangle; the name of the object is underlined and may optionally have the class name appended to it.

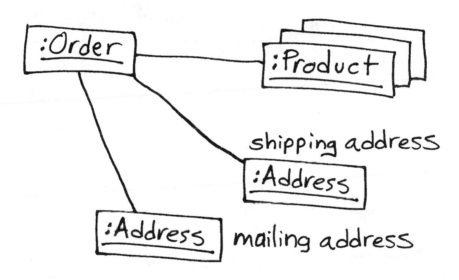

❹ **Collaboration Diagram**—an enhanced version of the object diagram. The object diagram shows objects and their links. The collaboration diagram shows objects and the messages that pass between them (the *reason* for the links).

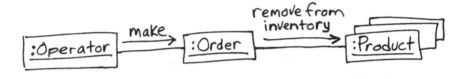

❺ **Sequence Diagram**—shows the sequence of message exchanges between objects.

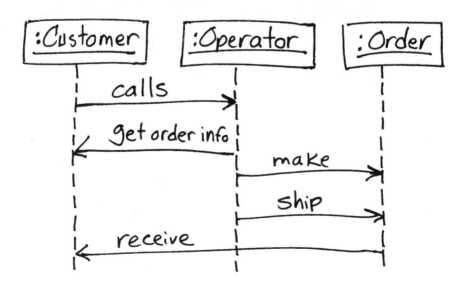

❻ **Statechart Diagram**—represents all the different states
a particular object can be in and the transitions between
those states.

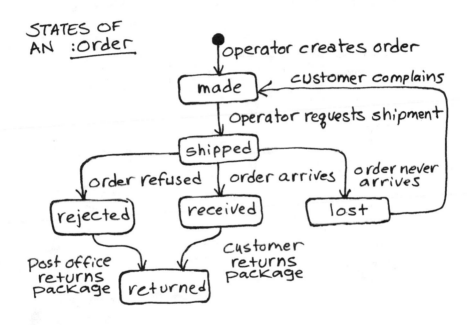

❼ **Activity Diagram**—similar to, but subtly different than a statechart diagram. Where the statechart diagram shows the transitions between states *of a single object*, the activity diagram shows a sequence of activities performed by one or more objects and how those activities affect the activities and states of other objects.

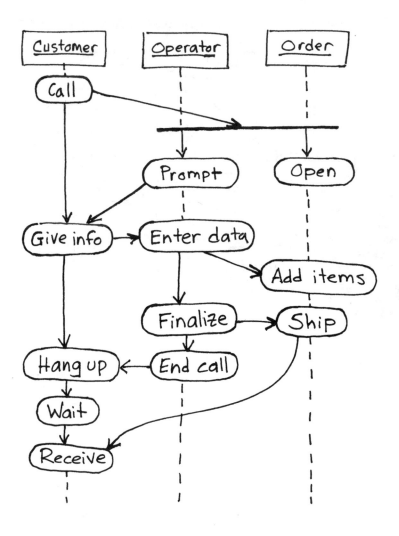

❽ **Component Diagram**—reflects the pieces that will make up the finished software system. This diagram represents both processes and subsystems.

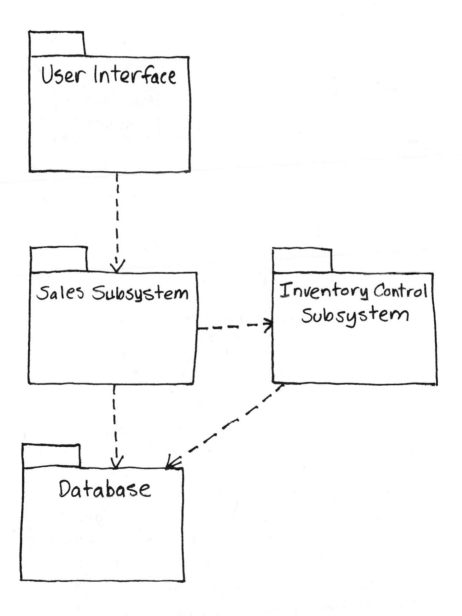

❾ **Deployment Diagram**—uses cubes to represent the relationships between the hardware elements of a system and the software elements of the system that run on each device.

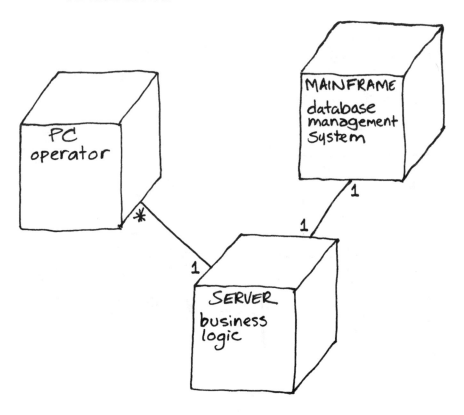

Software engineering is still a very young field. As such, many things are still under construction. UML is no exception. This is a very new diagramming technique and it still has some deficiencies. It is the first attempt by the software industry to agree on a set of standardized diagrams for representing software systems. Although at the time of this writing, UML has not been officially ratified, it is the *de facto* industry standard. UML is the fusion of the three main, competing software diagramming techniques (Booch, OMT, and OOSE) and replaces them. Any software design tools you invest in should be able to support UML.

THE ADVANCED CLASS

Alright, now we get to the hard stuff: You're only going to understand this section if you understood the rest of the chapter. Think of it as sort of a pop quiz.

OBJECT PERSISTENCE

So far our discussion of objects has only referred to objects as being entities that exist in the computer's main memory. Unfortunately, when you turn the power off on a computer everything in its main memory is lost, just like the way the glow of a light bulb filament is lost when you turn off a lamp. Therefore, for any type of software system to be useful, there must be a way to save its data to a permanent storage device, like a disk or tape. How useful would an accounts receivable program be if it lost all your accounts receivables every time the power went out or the system was rebooted. Persistent objects are objects that not only exist in the computers main memory, but that also have a mirror image in physical storage. There are a number of ways this can be accomplished. For example, the object can contain logic that saves any changes in its attributes to a relational database system before making the changes to the object in memory. A *relational database* is a database system that stores data in the form of tables. A table can be created for each class, with each attribute of each class represented as a column in the table; each row in the table contains the attribute *values* for a specific object.

Another way to achieve object persistence is to use an *object database*. Object databases create an exact mirror image of an object in storage on disk; not only are the values of the object's attributes saved to disk, but the object's relationships with other objects are preserved as well. If a particular object is retrieved from disk, the values of its attributes are restored in memory and the attribute values of any associated objects as well. For example, if a particular **bankCustomer** is referenced in an application, it will *automatically* be retrieved from the object database, along with its associated **checkingAccount**, **savingsAccount**, and **creditCardAccount** objects.

The advantages of using an object database over a relational database are:

❶ Unlike relational databases, the application program does not need to have any additional logic to mirror objects to an object database. Object databases provide a way to designate which objects in a program are to be persistent. These objects are then automatically mirrored to disk; the programmer does not need to write any additional code.

❷ Since, when an object is retrieved into memory from an object database, all associated objects are loaded into memory at the same instant, object databases can greatly outperform relational databases for applications where information is needed from several tables at the same time. So far, the telco, financial, and defense industries have been the biggest customers of object databases.

The disadvantages of object databases relative to relational databases are:

❶ Performance of requests for data that do not follow the physical ordering of objects on the disk can have atrocious performance. Today's object databases do not have the kinds of sophisticated techniques that relational databases use for extracting data out of order. For example, object databases would be pretty slow in telling you the names of each **bankCustomer** with balances less than $100.

❷ The technology is still very immature. The security, reliability, and data integrity features of most object databases are primitive by relational database standards—although their marketing departments will tell you otherwise.

❸ It is a lot easier for people to think of data being stored in tabular form—you can easily visualize the rows and columns of a spreadsheet in your mind. But what does an object look like? Even for programmers who are familiar with object-oriented programming, the concept of objects simultaneously existing in memory and on disk is a hard one to grasp. They ask questions like, "What do you mean I don't have to 'explicitly save data to disk'?" There is a little learning curve even though the way data is mirrored to an object database is actually easier.

❹ They do not support legacy applications well. An object database cannot be easily used as a data store for a non-object-oriented program.

A third approach that has become popular is relational databases with object-oriented extensions or *universal databases*. A universal database is one in which an entire object can be stored in a single field of a single row of data. These database systems still don't have the performance advantage of being able to load an object and all of its associated objects into memory at once, but they can provide the application programming ease of object databases. In addition, they can only take advantage of *some* of the random data extraction capabilities of relational databases. Remember: *All* the attributes of each object are stored in *one* column of a table—relational database systems are optimized for having *one* attribute represented by one column. Again, this will be less of an issue as the technology matures.

To date, neither object databases nor the universal database concept has really taken off. Many application developers still use relational tables or flat files to store the attribute values of their objects.

DISTRIBUTED OBJECTS

Distributed objects are an object-oriented attempt at simplifying the development of client-server systems. To understand what distributed objects are and what they can do for you, you have to understand a little bit about client-server systems.

A client-server system is made up of basically two parts: a *server* application and one or more *client* applications, as the name suggests. The client program is usually a program with a graphical user interface that is used by end-users. However, a client application can also be some kind of a program that doesn't deal with humans at all, like a program that adjusts some valve on a pipe connected to a nuclear reactor. The reason these programs are called *clients* is because they ask a server program running on the same or some remote machine to do something for them—fetch some data, do some calculation, provide instructions, etc. Here are some of the issues programmers face when implementing a client-server system:

✪ The server program has to be always up and running—it constantly listens for messages coming in from the client.

✪ In order for the server program to be able to receive messages from a client and send replies, it has to have complex communications code built in.

✪ The client also has to have complex communications code built-in in order to send and receive messages from the server.

✪ The server program has to have decision logic that tells it what to do with each type of request a client can make. For example, if a client requests a customer's account balance, the server has to have logic to understand that it is being asked to fetch an account balance, then it has to get the account balance and return it to the client.

✪ If there are going to be multiple clients, the server has to be able to keep track of which client is asking it for what.

✪ If the client is on a different kind of computer than the server, the server may have to have code in it to convert the data it sends to another format.

✪ Both the client and the server have to have logic to handle what happens when the communications link between them is lost.

Programming client-server applications is just plain hard. Surely there must be an easier way! This is exactly the problem distributed objects attempt to solve: hiding the complexity of client-server programming from the application programmer. The goal of distributed object architectures is to allow an object in one program to send a message to an object in another program. It doesn't matter what object-oriented language the second program is written in; whether the second program is running on the same machine as the first object or some machine on the other side of the world; or even what operating system the second program was written for. At least that's the theory anyway. The truth is, a distributed object system will only support as many platforms and languages as the vendor chooses to implement.

It is easiest to explain distributed objects by example. This example will also serve as a good example of how all the elements of an object-oriented system fit together. Suppose you have a GUI application that is used by your company's customer service department. When a customer calls in, the service rep enters their phone number and up pops their account information in detail. One of the other functions of the system is that it can tell the customer service rep whether it is OK to extend credit to the customer. The system that approves credit lines is actually located somewhere back at corporate headquarters on the same machine that holds all of the company's account and customer records. When the service rep is ready to obtain an approval for the customer's line of credit, they click on an "Approve" button, and an few seconds later either an approval or a rejection comes back.

Based on what you learned earlier in this chapter, you can probably guess that we want to represent customers and accounts
in the customer service program as objects. Customer objects
have two methods called **getAccounts()** and **approveCredit()**.
Let's focus on the **approveCredit()** method. Every time a customer service rep brings up a particular customer's information, a corresponding **customer** object is manufactured from
the **Customers** class inside the customer service system. When
the rep clicks on the "Approve" **button** object on the user interface, the **button**'s **click()** method sends a message to the current **customer** object to **approveCredit()**. When this method
gets invoked, what we really want to happen is for the server
program back at headquarters to execute its complex credit
approval logic and send us back either an approval or a rejection. One way a programmer could implement this system is to
write all the complex communication logic to get an approval
from the server into the **approveCredit()** method; the other
would be to use *distributed objects*.

In a distributed object scheme the **customer** object would be
nothing more than a façade, called a *proxy object*. A proxy
object looks just like any other object to the application programmer. You can even send it messages. However, the real
magic is that it has a partner object on the *server* that looks just
like it and performs work on its behalf on the server.

The thing that makes this magic possible is a piece of software
that sits between the object on the client system and the object
on the server system. This intermediary is an *object request*

brokering system. Any time a method is invoked on the proxy object, the object request brokering system takes over—it communicates the request to a method on the partner object on the server, monitors for completion of the request, then sends the result back to the proxy. *The application programmer is relieved of all responsibility for managing communications between the client and server—in fact, it is possible that the programmer may not even know where the server object is.* This is a huge reduction in the amount of effort required to develop a client-server application.

To continue with our previous example, when a customer's information is requested by a rep, a **customerProxy** object is created. When the rep clicks on the "Approve" **button** on the screen, the **button**'s **click()** method sends a message to the current **customerProxy** object to **approveCredit()**. Processing for the **approveCredit()** request is then passed on, via the object request brokering system, to the appropriate **customer** object on the server for processing. When the result comes back it is returned by the **customerProxy** to the **button**'s **click()** method, which in turn, posts the result to the display before it exits.

Congratulations! You now know more than most of your software development staff about object technology (and probably more than you ever *wanted* to know). Now lets get on to the good stuff.

4 WHERE'S THE BEEF?
(WHAT'S IN IT FOR YOU?)

"OK, big deal, so you've got some fancy new way of programming—what's in it for me?" In a word, the answer is *profits*. Used correctly, object technology has tremendous potential to improve your competitive advantage and reduce software development and maintenance overhead. Business today is as much about information as anything else and just having it is not enough. Competitive advantage comes from how you use it. In corporate Darwinism, the company that is the most adaptable to market changes and provides the best services is the one that survives and prospers.

Let's face it, the way software is developed today is a money pit. In a large company the annual expenditures for the care and feeding of programmers can easily exceed six figures per year *per programmer*—that's salary, benefits, training, office space, software, equipment and supplies, and human and machine resources to support them. It only makes sense to use them as efficiently as possible. Object technology can do this for you and a whole lot more. Object technology is about rapid, efficient deployment and adaptation of software systems.

REDUCED DEVELOPMENT COST

The art of programming as it is practiced today is one of the most resource-wasting processes in your business. Imagine if other groups in your company worked the way programmers do: The shipping department would pack and repack each order two or three times before shipping anything. There would always be a couple of secretaries typing exactly the same letter. No one would ever use clip-art or stock photos—all graphics would be produced from scratch. Down in manufacturing, every time someone completed a unit, someone else would come along and take a couple of screws off. You get the picture.

Object technology is as much a communication medium as it is a programming technique. It gives programmers an effective way to share information and work. On countless occasions, in a traditional development shop, programmers reinvent the wheel. In practice, a given programmer is very likely to rewrite the exact routine that was just written by another programmer elsewhere in the company—the larger the company, the more likely this is to occur. With object technology, if a programmer solves a particular problem and implements the solution in the form of a class or component, that solution has been effectively published: Any programmer faced with a similar problem can just plug the new class or component into their application. Not only does this save the programmer having to write the code again, but it also saves them having to *research* the problem again. Writing code doesn't really take all that long; figuring out *what* to write and where to put it can take months.

By sharing code, the total amount of code that is written across the organization can be greatly reduced—and it's a self-multiplying process. Each time a programmer writes a new piece of software, he or she uses some preexisting classes either purchased from an outside vendor or borrowed from the company's *class library*. He or she may create *new* classes for the project as well. The new classes are subsequently added to the company's inventory of stock classes, which further reduces the amount of new code that has to be written for future projects.

An additional benefit is that individual programmers can work more on developing depth of skill rather than breadth. The traditional programmer must be a jack-of-all-trades. Through object technology, an individual or group that specializes in a certain area can encapsulate that expertise in the form of objects and make it available to rest of the company. For example, suppose a group that has a lot of experience writing statistical routines creates a bunch of classes for the objects commonly used in statistical analysis. They can share these classes with programmers in other areas such as marketing, who do not have the math expertise to write statistics stuff.

Rather than spending weeks or months figuring out how to calculate some statistic, the programmers of the marketing application can just plug in statistics objects wherever they need them. Similarly, the decision support folks might be able to use some of the types of objects with which the marketing programmers work. This kind of class swapping allows the skills of various groups to be leveraged across the organization.

FASTER DEPLOYMENT OF NEW SYSTEMS

Information is money, and whoever gets the information first makes the most money. In other words, it pays to be the first kid on your block with the better mousetrap. One of the key benefits of object technology is that it helps you build new mousetraps and improve the ones you have much faster.

Because object-oriented programs can consist of reusable parts, the amount of time required to produce a given piece of software is greatly reduced. Once your library of classes, whether purchased or developed in-house, begins to take shape, programmers can rapidly piece together new software. This leads to much shorter development time for software, whether its intended users are internal or external. It should be noted, however, that in the beginning, object-oriented software projects might actually take a little longer. This price is acceptable though, when you consider that your first object-oriented project will form the basis for all projects to follow.

In a way, a class library is a physical manifestation of the learning curve. Every time a programmer creates a class of objects to deal with a certain type of problem, what that programmer learned along the way is embodied in the resulting classes. In subsequent projects, not only can the code be reused, but also the designs themselves. This is significant because, in the world of objects, the time required to design a program is far greater than the time required to write it. As with reuse of code, *design reuse* increases as the organization's class library grows, significantly reducing development time.

FASTER ADAPTATION AND ENHANCEMENT OF EXISTING SYSTEMS

The amount of time required to develop new code is nothing though, when you compare it to the time-per-line of code required to modify complex, existing applications. If it takes your software people what seems like an eternity to make relatively simple enhancements to your software, this is why. The problem is not how long it takes to write the code—enhancements are usually small relative to the overall size of a software system. It's how long it takes to figure *how to fit the new code in with what's already there.* The are several reasons for this:

✪ The person making the changes is most likely *not* the person who wrote the thing, so there is a learning curve.

✪ Even if the person making the changes *is* the same person that wrote the original code, he or she may have forgotten exactly how it works.

✪ It takes a long time to figure out what else is going to be *impacted* when you make a change in a complex program

✪ Since bugs in some systems can be fatal to the company or even to humans (e.g., the software on board the space shuttle), programmers have to exercise extreme caution when modifying mission critical systems

Changing complex, object-oriented systems is usually much easier than modifying traditional systems. Because all activity in an object-oriented program is centered around objects, it's usually a lot easier to figure out what needs to be changed. Suppose, for example, you wanted to assess a service charge every time a customer exceeds their charge account limit. There are two classes of objects here: **Customer** and **Charge-Account**. The only one that needs to be modified, however, is the **ChargeAccount** class—it's the class of objects that has the

creditLimit attribute and that will receive the service charge. In addition, the only thing that really has to change is the way the **ChargeAccount** class performs its **makeCharge()** behavior.

The *encapsulation* provided by objects also reduces the amount of time required to modify existing systems. As long as the way other objects in the system *interface* with a given class of objects doesn't change, most code modifications can be isolated to that class. This is similar to putting a more energy-efficient bulb in a light socket. The new bulb screws in the same way as the old one and puts out exactly the same amount and quality of light; no changes to the light socket are required whatsoever. The only thing that changes is the internal design of the bulb.

Even if a class interface change *is* required, the scope of the changes will probably be limited. Most likely, the only classes of objects affected will be ones that rely on the behaviors that changed in the modified class. Returning to the **Charge-Account** example, the *only* change required in the *entire system* is to modify the **makeCharge()** method so that it adds a service charge to the **accountBalance** attribute when the sum of the new charge amount and the **accountBalance** exceeds the **creditLimit** value. **Customer** objects will still provide *exactly the same information* they always have when they ask their associated **ChargeAccount** objects to **makeCharge()**. The only change will be in *how* the **ChargeAccount** objects *process* the **makeCharge()** request.

Another time factor in enhancing legacy applications is debugging. Because it is virtually impossible for any one person to consider all the ramifications of a change in a complex program, changing legacy applications often results in bugs. It may take days, weeks, months, or in some cases years to track down all of the bugs introduced by a relatively simple enhancement. Is it any wonder there is much wailing and gnashing of teeth every time you ask for something simple like the ability to record dates after the year 1999?

Not only do object-oriented programming techniques greatly reduce the likelihood of introducing bugs, but also they greatly simplify the process of finding them. To find a bug, the programmer starts by simply looking at the *thing* that isn't acting right. For example, if someone's charge-account balance was calculated incorrectly, the first place to look for the bug is the **ChargeAccount** object.

LOWER HEAD COUNT

Producing software is an expensive proposition, and the most expensive aspect of it is the labor. Object technology not only allows you to get the most out of your people, it allows you to get by with *less* people. Much of the savings come from the way object-oriented programming techniques simplify complex software systems.

As we discussed in previous sections, in large, traditional software systems it is very hard for any one individual to completely understand the entire system. This problem gets worse as time goes on. Eventually there is only a handful of old timers who really have any clue at all, and they're not completely sure. This is an extremely bad position to be in because it encourages empire building, creates an unhealthy dependence on one or a few individuals, and makes it very difficult to get new people trained. Even if you do manage to get them trained, the odds of keeping them any length of time (if they have any ambition at all) are very slim—being a maintenance programmer in someone else's code empire is just no fun. As a result, the turnaround times for software enhancements and bug fixes just get longer and longer.

Companies frequently take a brute force approach to dealing with this problem: They just keep throwing bodies at the problem. Executives scream, "Faster! Faster!" Software managers scream back, "We need more people! We need more people!" The programmers scream "We're over worked! We're over worked!" So eventually, management sends in more people. That's kind of like sending more cooks into the kitchen because dinner's taking too long. The result is that you get one cook stirring the pot, one adding the pepper, one adding the garlic, and so on. Pretty soon, they're stepping all over each other, doing each other's jobs, and fighting over who gets to do what. Dinner doesn't really come out any faster—in fact, it may take longer and definitely cost more. This really happens in software development! The problem is not the number of cooks, it's the recipe. If you choose ingredients that cook slow, your meal will take a long time to cook. It simply takes *time* to figure out how to make changes to a complex system.

There are only two ways to deal with the problem.

❶ You keep hiring people until each conceivable task is being worked on by a single individual, or

❷ you do something to make the software easier to work on.

As we saw in the previous section, that's where object technology comes in. By creating programs that are systems of components rather than big globs of code, the programs are easier to understand and you can get away with fewer bodies. In addition, code that is easy to understand and modify discourages empire building (if everyone understands it, who has an empire?) and makes it a lot easier to train new people and replace old ones lost through attrition.

Purchasing components is another opportunity for savings. Buying code from other companies allows you to write a lot less code in-house and acquire specialized code without having to hire the experts required to write it. For example, consider an application that is going to transmit data continuously between satellite stores and the home office. You can acquire the necessary software for handling the data transmissions by either

✪ hiring an expensive software developer with this specialty for more than a $100,000 per year,

✪ paying to have one of your people trained for a few thousand bucks, or

✪ if your system is object-oriented, by purchasing a class
   library from a vendor that specializes in data communications for less than $2000.

As you can see, by choosing the last option, you can get what
you need for a fraction of the cost of the other two options. This
is because the cost of development is now distributed over
all the vendor's customers. Whether code is purchased exter-
nally or developed internally, object-oriented programming
techniques greatly simplify the job of writing, learning, and
maintaining software systems—and that translates to less
ducks on the pond.

IMPROVE QUALITY

Software defects are expensive, both in the labor required to fix
them and in the problems they cause. In the best case, they
cause someone a little extra work; in the worst case, they can
result in fines, missed deadlines, lawsuits, downtime, lost business, lost money, and in some cases, lost lives. (How embar-
rassing would that be to have explain on national TV why you
lost 10 employees when the robot that makes the donut holes
decided it was tired of just making holes in donuts?) Using
object technology will not guarantee that your software will be
free of defects, but it's the best bug repellent available today.

Object-oriented programming techniques help prevent bugs by protecting data, forcing programmers to do better design work, and by facilitating reuse of proven code. The mechanism for protecting data in object-oriented software is encapsulation (data-hiding). The theory is simple and it works: If you can't see the data, you can't screw it up. However, the one thing you can't hide data from is bad design. Just like anything else, if a program is poorly designed, it will be of poor quality. Object technology can't save you from this.

The object-oriented way of programming creates an environment in which programmers *must* design before they code. In traditional programming, programmers can just start hacking away before they really understand the problem. This usually results in numerous patch jobs as the project progresses. The object-oriented programmer is forced to do a better job of analysis. If the programmer doesn't at least have some idea of what objects are needed in a given program, the programmer has no idea what to begin coding. In fact, by taking the time to think through the design, the programmer may discover no coding is needed at all. The classes he or she is looking for may already be in the library.

Even in unstructured and structured programming, reuse of proven routines is a good way to reduce the number of bugs. The more places you reuse a procedure, the more likely it is that bugs will be found in testing rather than production. Also, a procedure that proves to be error-free in one application, will most likely be free of errors in any other application you use it.

The same logic applies to the use of classes. Also, because object-oriented programming languages contain features that help programmers reuse code, it is more likely that programmers will take advantage of proven classes.

A last aspect of software quality often taken for granted is *usability*. A program that is rock-solid-reliable, but hard to use and learn, can be as damaging as a program that is full of bugs. There is an old saying in the computer business: Garbage in, garbage out. In other words, no matter how reliable a program is, if users supply it with bad data, the results will be bad as well. The more assistance a program provides to the user, the less likely the user will provide bad input.

One of the greatest advances in software usability has been the *graphical user interface* (GUI). Part of the reason for the proliferation of programs with GUIs has been object technology. Prior to object-oriented programming's recent popularity, creating applications with a GUI was an unbelievable amount of work. Now programmers can just create GUI applications by visually piecing together ready-made components (objects) using programs called *visual builders*. Programming tasks that used to take weeks now take hours or even minutes. This seems to be the direction that all programming, not just GUI applications, is headed. The net result for us all is software that is less expensive to produce and easier to use.

ENABLE VENDORS AND CUSTOMERS

One final way that object technology can help your business is as an enabling technology. Depending on what kind of business you're in, it might be desirable to have your customers or vendors directly hooked into your systems. For example, if you run a manufacturing operation, it might be advantageous to have your inventory management system tied directly to your parts suppliers. Conversely, if your business is supplying parts to manufacturers, you might want your customers' inventory systems tied to your order-processing systems. In either scenario, with traditional software development you might have to develop some kind of complex protocol for communication between your systems and theirs.

Using object technology it is possible to provide the vendor or customer with the software components they need to directly interface with your systems or build systems that are actually just extensions of your own systems. For example, you could give your customer or supplier the class libraries that contain classes for representing data in the format your systems expect it to be in, for communicating with your systems, and for initiating transactions. The easier you make it for someone to do business with you, the more likely they will.

Well by now, hopefully, you're feeling pretty *bullish* about object technology. Used correctly, object technology is a strategic investment with very high potential returns. It can benefit the quality and range of services provided to both your internal and external customers. In addition, it can improve your ability to respond, adapt, merge, and grow, while at the same time reducing your software development costs. However, as with any other power tool, handle with caution and always wear protective gear. Like a friend of mine always says, "If you mess with the bull, you get the horn." Now that you know all the good stuff, flip to the next chapter to see all the potential gotchas.

5 WATCH YOUR STEP
(Now the Bad News)

"Hurry, hurry, hurry . . . step right up right up folks . . .
  the medicine show is in town !**"**

In a lot of ways the object pushers are a lot like the medicine men of the Old West. They roll into town with their brightly painted wagons and give you all kinds of song and dance to sell their miracle cures. It's only after your pockets are empty and the dust has blown over the wagon tracks that you find out whether their patent medicine is really going to work. The sad reality is that object technology often fails to live up to the promises. In a few cases, it actually kills the patient. So far we've only discussed the good things about objects; let's take a look at the dark side of object technology and how to avoid suffering its ill effects.

DON'T COUNT ON ANYTHING

The strangest thing happens in the computer industry: Ordinarily rational people make incredibly stupid decisions based on what everybody else is doing. The best advice I can give you on when and when not to use object technology is *think for yourself!* Don't be swayed by the trade press, don't be swayed by consultants, and don't be swayed by your own people. Object technology is not perfect, it's not for everybody, and it doesn't work in all situations.

Rule 1: Be a skeptic. Question everything and everyone.

The key to knowing when and when not to invest in object technology is the same as the key to knowing when and when not to invest in anything: good analysis. Understand all of the costs and the benefits. Know

✪ how much of your existing systems will have to be rewritten,

✪ how much retraining is needed,

✪ what you will have to spend on consultants and contractors, and

✪ how much of the code can be purchased from outside vendors.

Object technology may not be for you if

- ✪ all of your applications are small and you don't have many of them.

- ✪ implementing software changes happens at an acceptable rate and bugs are rare.

- ✪ you seldom need to develop new applications.

- ✪ you run your business with vendor-written software.

If what you have is really working for you, it may not be worth the cost to change. Object technology is best suited to companies that have complex systems that need to be constantly enhanced or changed.

You are probably a good candidate for object technology if

- ✪ there are always a lot of bugs in your systems.

- ✪ it takes your IT department a long time to fix bugs.

- ✪ it seems to take forever for your IT department to make changes.

- ✪ no matter how many programmers you hire, it never seems to be enough.

✪ you are doing some business process or systems reengineering.

If you do make the decision to move to object technology, assess whether your existing personnel are the right people to implement it. "My programmers are top notch. They've all been with me for fifteen years, so they should be able to handle this object stuff, right?" Wrong. One of the most common ways companies blow themselves out of the water with object technology is they assume the same old people will be able to figure it out and do it right. Survey says: No! The initial tendency of people with a heavy background in structured or unstructured programming is to do things the way they've always done it with a few objects mixed in for fun. This is a recipe for disaster. You can end up with code that is *worse* than what you had before.

Along those same lines, the most critical decision you can make is who will be the chief architect. A common mistake companies make is to make the chief architect someone who was a senior programmer on their legacy systems. This is a whole different ball game, folks. He or she may have been a genius with your old systems, but object-oriented programming requires a whole new way of thinking about software. Your *senior* programmer just became a freshman with a whole lot of bad habits to unlearn. The only person qualified to be the chief architect is someone with a *proven record of success* in object-oriented analysis and design.

Rule 2: If Bo don't know objects, Bo don't know diddley.

YOU HAVE TO CRAWL FIRST

"Alright Marsha, we've just spent $2,213,324,423.95 on teaching your people C++, we bought the !@#! CASE tool you asked for, we hired the consultants, now we don't care what you do, just get those object things into that system!"

The most dangerous thing a group that's new to object technology can do is to rush into it and try it out on a major project. There are all kinds of horror stories about outrageously expensive object-oriented software systems that were delivered late, over budget, and dead on arrival. Almost universally these stories are about some organization's first attempt at object-oriented software development. Never, never, *never* make a mission-critical system your first object-oriented project. You will fail. It doesn't matter how good your people are or how big a deal the consultant is. Unless you plan to fire everybody and start over from scratch with a staff of experts, don't even think about it. Even if you *did* try the scorched earth approach, you'd probably *still* fail because the new people won't know enough about your business.

Why are the first few projects such a big deal? Object-oriented programming is just not something people get right away— especially old-school programmers, because object technology takes everything they ever learned and turns it inside out. It looks similar, but it's not, and that's where the danger lies.

Anyone can learn an object-oriented programming language fairly quickly. However, learning to think in terms of objects is another thing entirely. Experience shows it takes a veteran programmer about six months to get it and years to master it.

Rule 3: Your first object-oriented development projects should be non–mission-critical, non-ambitious applications.

LIVING WITH THE LEGACY

Another way that companies get themselves into trouble is by trying to mix objects in with legacy systems. There are some people out there who will tell you this is a great thing to do. It can be done, and in a very special set of circumstances it can make the code better, but it usually just makes things worse.

Almost every programming language available, including, believe it or not, COBOL, has been extended with object-oriented features. There is an overwhelming temptation for programmers to use some of these features just to try them out. With few exceptions, mixing structured and object-oriented code creates code that is more complex than what was there before, and that has none of the benefits of object technology. Especially if the new code was introduced by someone who doesn't understand object-oriented programming.

Legacy software isn't the only legacy that you have to be concerned with. The other is legacy skill. Don't try to introduce object technology into your mission-critical applications unless you are willing to retrain *everybody*. Most companies just appoint a couple of gurus to go take the class and come back and teach everybody else. This is a mistake because if they begin introducing object-oriented code into the system, they will be the only people who understand it. Also, because the developers with traditional programming skills don't understand the new code, they will put up fierce resistance. As a matter of fact, getting legacy programmers to buy in may be one of the toughest challenges you face. The greatest challenge in achieving *any* cultural change is always getting buy-in, and getting your people to adopt object technology may be the toughest challenge you've ever faced. It's on a par with trying to get someone to accept a new religion, and realistically without a strong, respected champion, you don't have a prayer.

Rule 4: Don't put object-oriented code into legacy systems unless: 1) The person doing it is an expert, 2) there is a really, really, *really* good excuse to do it, and 3) everyone who has to use and maintain the new code is trained in object-oriented programming.

FAT AND LAZY

Object technology is sort of like that fat cousin you're always trying to get married off. He has a great personality, but takes up a lot of space on the couch and doesn't win many footraces. One cost of object technology that is seldom discussed is the effect it has, directly or indirectly, on the size and performance of software systems.

Be prepared. Your hot new object-oriented application may not be as svelte and perform as well as its traditional counterparts. Some of this has to do with object programming languages themselves—the choice of language has a lot to do with performance and storage consumption. In object-oriented programming, the language is doing more of the work, and you pay for that in the size and execution speed of the program. Also, there is a cost associated with all the communication that goes on between objects. Every time one object uses another's method, the computer has to do some extra work. There is equivalent overhead in structured programs when one procedure calls another procedure. However, it happens more frequently in object-oriented programs.

Object-oriented software is typically larger than conventional software because of the extensive reuse of code. When a new subclass is created, it usually doesn't use *all* of the member data inherited from the parent class. Nonetheless, an object created from the subclass must use enough of the computer's memory to accommodate all of its attributes, plus *all* of the attributes of the parent class. This is especially true of code purchased from class-library and framework vendors. After numerous generations of inheritance, there can be quite a few unused data items. In programs that instantiate hundreds or thousands of objects from a given class, this excess baggage can use up quite a bit of memory. As a result, the disk storage and memory requirements of object-oriented programs can be significantly greater than their traditional counterparts.

Memory usage also impacts performance. Most modern computers use something called *virtual memory*. Using virtual memory means that when the computer's *real* (electronic) memory is filled to the brim with programs and data, the computer will start to overflow the least-recently-used programs and data from real memory to disk. When an item that was swapped to disk is needed again, it is pulled back into real memory and something else is moved to the disk. The more memory consumed on the system, the more frequently this swapping (called paging) takes place. A computer's disk drives are literally more than a thousand times slower than its electronic memory, so you can imagine the impact this has on the speed with which programs run.

The extent to which object-oriented programs are bigger depends on the quality of the original design. A well-designed parent class is minimized to the common essentials of all child classes, so there is little excess baggage. Nonetheless, be advised that using object-oriented software may require you to upgrade your hardware.

If object-oriented software is so "fat and lazy," why does any-body want to use it? It's a classic software engineering trade-off: storage *vs.* performance *vs.* maintainability. The reasoning is that, because the cost of upgrading processors, memory, and disk drives at today's prices is trivial compared to the cost of servicing bugs and adding enhancements to complex software systems, maintainability should be the primary concern. Also, for many programs the size and performance differences are not important. For example, if your company only has a thousand employees and you don't plan to grow, it's really not going to matter (within reason) how big or fast the program that lets you look up people's telephone extensions is. Remember too, that by reengineering legacy applications, you often get rid of a lot of extraneous code. As a result, *the object-oriented code may actually be smaller and more efficient.*

Rule 5: Think. The biggest gains in performance and savings in system resources (and consequently, money) come from brilliant solutions, not the programming technique being used.

IT JUST TAKES TIME

Design time in early projects will be much longer than for traditional programming methods, and with good reason. In traditional programs, flawed design can cause projects to be overdue and over budget, but design errors in object-oriented software are much more serious because of the extensive reuse of code. Just as a bad mold will produce bad mechanical parts, poorly designed classes produce flawed objects in every program in which they are used. In addition, design flaws in a given class will be inherited by any subclasses derived from it. In the worst case, bad object code may not be reusable at all and may necessitate starting from scratch late in a project.

If your organization is new to object technology, you also need to figure in time for the learning curve. There will be a lot of code rewrites when your people first start using object technology. It's almost impossible to get it right the first time you do it, no matter how many books you read and no matter how many classes you go to.

Rule 6: When you finally do take on the first mission-critical project with object technology, invest the time to design it correctly. If you do not invest in good design, game over. An object-oriented software project that is poorly designed will not only hurt you now, but it will hurt you in the future on all subsequent projects that inherit from the code. At best, poorly-designed object code won't be reusable— which, of course, sort of defeats the purpose. The worst case is that the code in the first project will have to be scrapped and rewritten from scratch.

VANISHING CLASSES

Classes need to be protected and managed just like any other business resource. You need a system of inventory management and a way to let programmers know what classes are in the inventory. Otherwise, you risk losing your investment.

Programmers can only reuse code if they know it exists. The larger your inventory of classes or components gets, the harder it is for people to know what's in it, especially when the library is being populated by multiple development organizations. Therefore, it is in your best interest to invest in a system to manage your class *library*. Imagine what would happen to your business if you didn't have an inventory management system to track inventory or a personnel system to track human resources.

You have millions of dollars invested in your mission-critical software. You can't afford to pay for things twice. If a programmer can't find the class for a needed part easily or doesn't know it exists, he or she will just create the class all over again for his or her own use—and that kind of defeats the purpose of using object technology in the first place.

Rule 7: Software components are information assets. They should be tracked, managed, and inventoried just like any other mission critical data. This is the only way to get your money's worth out of reusable software components. If you don't know you have it or where it is, then it's like you never had it at all.

6 THE ROUND UP
(STAFFING FOR OBJECT TECHNOLOGY)

So you've decided to take the bull by the horns and ride the object technology beast after all. Well, you best round yerself up some top-notch wranglers to give you a hand, then. More so than with any other kind of software development, the key to a successful transition to object technology is having the right people. If your organization lacks skill and experience in object-oriented programming, then it's a good idea to look outside for help. While training goes a long way toward getting your people up to speed, there is no substitute for experience. There are a few different places you can go for help: new hires, contractors, and consultants. There's no shortage of people out there claiming to be object technology experts; the trick is to find the ones who really are.

OLD DOGS, NEW TRICKS

The main thing to remember, regardless of the source you use for outside skill, is that programming experience doesn't necessarily mean *object-oriented* programming experience. There is great temptation when looking to hire contractors or regular employees to go with the people who have the most programming experience. For traditional programming jobs this is often, but not always, a good rule of thumb. However, when staffing for object technology, years of programming experience is irrelevant—in fact, a strong background in structured programming can actually be a bad thing.

The most important thing to look for in outside help is the actual amount of experience *working with object technology and a successful track record doing it*. It's better to hire a programmer with only three years' work experience, all of which is in object-oriented programming, than someone with fifteen years' programming experience, only six months of which is with objects. Object-oriented analysis, design, and programming is something you only get good at by doing a lot; an extensive background in traditional programming will not help you at all.

Why is a background in object-oriented programming so critical? As mentioned in the previous chapter, if an object-oriented design is flawed, it may be necessary to rewrite parts from scratch . . . and if an object-oriented system happens to be developed with the waterfall design methodology commonly used by traditional systems architects, these kind of fatal errors probably won't surface until very late in the project. Experienced object-oriented architects use a process called *iterative development* that allows critical design flaws to be caught earlier and fixed before they're extensively reused. But it's more than just the way object-oriented architects work; it's also the way they *think*. Learning to write programs that include objects is easy; learning the right objects to include is very hard—especially if you are used to thinking of software systems in terms of the machine functions they perform rather than in terms of the *things* the system is supposed to represent.

Speaking of old dogs, don't forget your current people—you know, the folks who are experts in your business, the ones who are going to teach all these outsiders the insides of your business model. No matter what you do, invest in training 100 percent of the people who are involved with your current systems. You can hire the world's best consultants, contractors, and new hires to come in and build the most perfect, elegant, elaborate object-oriented system, and have it completely destroyed over the long term by one legacy programmer who "don't see why we gotta have all this object-oriented !@#$ in the first place since it really ain't no different than we've been doin' all along anyway, 'cept they just use a bunch of big, fancy new words and such." Also, be sure that the training does not come too far in advance of when they're actually going to start using what they've learned; object-oriented programming is definitely one of those things that if you don't use it, you lose it. One of the fastest ways to throw money away on object technology training is to spend eight hundred to fifteen hundred dollars (not including travel expenses) per head to send your people to classes six months before the project begins. No, the class handouts won't help.

HIRING CONSULTANTS

Consultants are usually very expensive and quite often not worth it. For your first object-oriented project in particular, you really need someone who'll be there on a daily basis during development. For that, a good contractor is most often the more cost-effective solution. In this book, a *consultant* is someone who basically does no implementation and for the most part, only gives advice or does high-level design work. A *contractor* is someone who provides the full range of services from analysis to design to implementation. The distinction is necessary because often in the industry the terms *consultant* and *contractor* are used interchangeably.

If you have your heart set on hiring a consultant, one thing to watch out for is that many of them are faking their expertise in object technology. Many big-name consultants made their mark during structured programming's golden years, and haven't written a line of code since. They make their money giving talks and publishing newsletters. Nonetheless, when the object bandwagon rolled by, as a matter of survival, they hopped on. So even though they're preaching it, they've never practiced it. As mentioned before, object technology is something you only get good at by doing.

It's very likely that the consultant who served you brilliantly on your structured programming projects will dig your grave on your object-oriented ones. You should only select consultants who have recent, documented successes with object-oriented projects. In addition, request references and follow up on them. There are some good object-oriented consultants out there, but you really have to work hard to find them.

BEWARE OF BROKERS

The way most people hire programming contractors today is through so called *brokers*. While these are good sources to get bodies from fast, you should look very carefully at what you're getting. The client reps from brokerage houses are often hired more for their ability to sell than for their technical ability. As a result, the people who are finding your contractors for you are most likely not qualified to screen them—and many of them *don't care*. They only make money when they sell you someone, so they often over-hype candidates. For this reason, only get object-oriented contractors from sources you trust, brokers who have built a reputation with you for delivering quality people. If you are new to using contract labor, ask your friends at other companies who they trust and recommend.

Each contractor should be screened at least as carefully as a permanent employee, no matter how highly recommended the person comes, no matter how impressive the person's resume is. Not only does the broker not have the expertise to properly screen candidates, but in a way, it's not in their best interest. The more bodies a broker has in the field, the more money the broker makes. As a result, basics, like checking references, are often skipped. This will be especially true if there is a very high demand for contractors in your geographic area.

Also, brokers love to recruit recent graduates; they get them cheaper. This is not necessarily a bad thing. Most graduates coming out of computer science and management information systems programs today have been trained in object-oriented techniques and their level of enthusiasm is a lot higher than seasoned veterans. They make some of the best worker bees. However, these are not the people you want as your systems architects.

When hiring object-oriented contractors, you should only solicit brokers after you have a very clear idea of what you want and what you want to pay. Then shop around; know the market. Like any other resource, the best way to obtain object-oriented contractors is on a negotiated contract. Especially in an arcane field like object technology, brokers try charge whatever they can get away with—sometimes as much as 75 percent mark-up over what they pay the consultant. When you negotiate the contract, ask them specifically what their mark-up is. Also, in case you find a keeper, be sure the contract includes terms for hiring the contractor away after a specified period of time. Many agencies charge a hefty hiring fee if you don't.

One final thing to consider is the fit of the contractor with the group you are hiring him or her for. If your company is new to object technology, the biggest obstacle you face is cultural change, not technology. If the person you bring in to help introduce the new culture is not accepted by the group, then most likely, object technology will not be accepted either. Any contractor should not only be screened by the hiring line manager, but by the team as well.

PERMANENT HIRES

If your organization presently has no object-oriented skills whatsoever, your best plan might be to recruit a few permanent hires who do. Unlike consultants and contractors, at the end of development they'll still (most likely) be around to provide continuity and to help with the maintenance—and the maintenance phase is what you should have in mind when you hire.

The most expensive time in the life of a software system is the maintenance phase. Development is easy: You make up the rules as you go. Fixing bugs and adding new functionality to an existing system is hard and very resource-intensive. This is especially true if the programmers charged with maintaining the system are not from the same team that developed the system. Taking over an existing piece of software is like moving to a brand new town: You don't know where anything is and you don't even know who to ask for directions. Many programs have as many lines of code as an encyclopedia has lines of text. Imagine trying to find something in an encyclopedia that has no page numbers, no index, no table of contents, and no particular order to the articles. The articles may either be clearly written or unbelievably cryptic. That's exactly what its like to work on a large software project—object-oriented or not.

Whether you use contract labor or permanent hires, at least *some* of the team that will be maintaining the new system *must* be involved in every phase of the development, from design to implementation. The absolute worst thing you could do is bring in a team of contractors to build the new object-oriented system while the old team of permanent employees continues to work on the legacy systems. This is what programmers call "throwing it over the wall," and it is a recipe for disaster:

✪ The team that writes the code has no accountability. Because they are not going to be the ones to maintain the system, they skimp on documentation and clarity of code just to get the work done faster. Programmers are lazy unless there is some incentive for them not to be.

✪ The team that has to maintain the code (the dirty work) will feel a great deal of resentment because they did not get to be involved in the creating the software (the fun part), plus they will have no ownership.

✪ The maintenance team will also feel cheated because they did not get to experiment with the new object-oriented stuff.

✪ Because the maintenance team will have to learn object-oriented programming techniques as they go, not only will they have to figure out where everything is in the "encyclopedia," they will have to learn the language it's written in as well.

If your regular employees don't quit under conditions like this, they will at the very least not be happy campers. Plus, you are guaranteed to have bugs galore when they get in and actually start to modify the code. Maintenance, as with development, of object-oriented code is a little different from the way things are traditionally done. Even though object code is generally easier to understand than its structured and unstructured counter-parts, it still takes a while to figure it out. The bottom line is: Have people on the development project who are going to be there to maintain the system.

For general-purpose coders, you might want to take the cue from the brokers and hire recent college graduates. They've been trained in object-oriented programming and their code is usually well-documented. However, for your systems architects, invest in the best professional hires you can find. Specifically, they should be senior-level programmers with substantial experience in object-oriented analysis, design, and development. Especially with the architect types, the whole team should be involved in the hiring decision; if the development team rejects the leader, they will probably reject object technology as well.

More importantly, they should have a proven record of success. Just because someone was an "architect" on a previous object-oriented development project doesn't mean that person knew what he or she was doing. If all of the person's experience prior to that project was in structured programming, it's very likely he didn't. Check references and always ask the question, "Would you hire this person again?" Pay close attention to how they answer.

THE BUY-VERSUS-BUILD DECISION

One of the really great things about object-oriented programming is the way solutions can be packaged up as libraries of reusable components. As a result, it is now possible to buy complex parts of software systems that you would previously have had to build in house. For example, imagine that you are trying to build a client-server system whose components communicate using the TCP/IP protocol (whatever *that* is). One approach would be to spend more than a hundred thousand dollars a year for a contractor or regular hire who is an expert in TCP/IP to do the communications piece of the system and give them six months to a year to make it all work; the other would be to buy communications components in the form of a *framework* or *class library* from an outside vendor for less than two thousand dollars. Your existing object-oriented programmers can then just plug the components right in to the system and start using them immediately. There is pretty much a canned solution available for every kind of business problem you can imagine: statistical analysis, multi-database access, user interface components, etc. In the case of the client-server system, you would also have the option of using *distributed objects* (discussed in Chapter 3) to further reduce the programming effort.

A word of caution on purchasing prefabricated software components: They are only as good as the company that makes them. Be sure that the vendor is a reliable company that will be around a while—get references just as you would for an employee. Also, try to only buy class libraries that include *all* the source code. This is important in case your team needs to make custom modifications or the company that sold you the components goes out of business, leaving you to maintain the class library yourself. You don't want to be in the position of having all your systems based on components that you can't get anyone to fix if there is a problem. In general, however, your people should *never* modify a vendor's software directly. If customization has to be done, your object-oriented programmers should use the classes in the vendor's class library to create new classes (subclasses). The needed modifications can then be done to the subclasses without making a single change to the components shipped by the vendor. This is the correct approach to take with object-oriented software: You don't have to worry as much about redoing your custom modifications if the vendor comes out with a new version of the class libraries, and it will be far easier for the vendor to help you if there are bugs.

So as you can see, there are a number of staffing (or *not*-staffing) options if you want to make the leap into object technology. The most important issue, no matter how you chose to staff for object technology, is change management. In fact, if you really won't be happy unless you hire a consultant, it would be better to invest in one who is an expert in change management or organizational behavior than in object technology. The key to your success in object technology is to have one hundred percent buy-in and 100 percent retraining for your current staff. Also, you as an executive have to champion object technology and advocate it as you would any other important strategic technology initiative. You can bring in the best people and the best technology money can buy, but if the existing crew isn't sold on it, you're better off just using the money for a huge, company-wide beer bash. *Esprit de corps* will be better at least. . . .

7 PLOWSHARES AND FERTILIZER
(THE TOOLS OF THE TRADE)

So now you've rustled yourself up a bunkhouse full of top-drawer wranglers: Let's get 'em saddled up and ready to ride! In software development, as in any other trade, a good portion of the return on personnel investment comes from giving people the right tools. How productive would the production line be if they still used handsaws instead of power saws? How would it impact your work if your secretary was still using a manual typewriter instead of a computer? This is especially true of object technology—getting the most out of your investment will depend to a great extent on what technology you choose to exploit it. Just using an object-oriented programming language is not enough. To be effective, an object-oriented development team needs tools for design, development, and software asset management.

CASE TOOLS

The first task in object-oriented development is to analyze and plan the system. Like any other kind of project, in object-oriented development the quality of the plans directly determine the quality, delivery dates, and cost of the final product. *Computer Aided Software Engineering (CASE)* tools not only help object-oriented developers lay out the design and determine the size of the work to be done, but many CASE tools will actually do some of the programming too.

For the most part, a CASE tool is nothing more than a highly overrated drafting program. In Chapter 3, we looked at nine very simple examples of UML diagrams used by software architects to design systems. In practice, complex software systems can consist of hundreds or even thousands of interacting objects. The diagrams representing these systems are extremely intricate; in other words, bar napkins and ballpoint pens only get you so far. At a certain level of detail, just as with any other type of design or engineering, it's time to enlist the help of a computer to do the drafting. Therefore, the first job of any object-oriented CASE tool is to help systems architects capture their ideas on "paper."

Another feature that CASE tools provide is assistance in managing constant revisions to complex diagrams. Object-oriented software development usually follows what is called an iterative or incremental development process. The way it works is that object-oriented designers do some high-level analysis, then a little design work, then write a little code to try some ideas out, then do a little bit of tinkering or testing with the code. Inevitably, problems with the design are found or users see prototypes and want more features or changes in the features they already asked for, so the designers go back and do a little more analysis, then a little more design, write some more code, and round and round she goes. . . . Because of this highly dynamic style of development, the diagrams documenting an object-oriented system design are in a constant state of flux. Pull one symbol out, reconnect a few lines, add a symbol or two here and there, etc. The CASE tool must not only manage all the visual changes, but also manage dependencies and relationships between design elements: "If we delete that widget over there, then those three other thing-a-muh-bobs have to be deleted as well."

A final function essential to a good CASE tool is the ability to generate object-oriented code automatically. One of the unique features of object-oriented programming is that the objects created in the design phase can be directly translated into actual objects in the system. When a structural engineer draws up plans for a suspension bridge, after the plans are done, all of the materials have to be ordered or manufactured and then assembled into the actual bridge. In software systems, on the other hand, nothing exists in the real world—it's all just machine instructions. So once a class and all its attributes, behaviors, and interactions with other classes has been completely described by the designer, some if not all of the code can be generated directly from the design by the CASE tool. The CASE tool gives graphical representations of classes and objects—the essential elements of an object-oriented program are really just a textual representation of the graphical design. Translating between the two is not that big a deal. For instance, this is how a class is represented in UML:

This is the corresponding representation in C++ code:

```
class Account {
    public
        void Debit (float Amount);
        void Credit (float Amount);
    private
        float Balance;
};
```

One recommendation on selecting a CASE tool: Be sure to get one that supports Unified Modeling Language (UML) diagrams. This appears to be the direction the entire industry is going for object-oriented design. While UML is far from perfect, it is the closest thing to a standard the industry currently has. Moreover, because it derives (or in object-speak, it *inherits*) from the three leading schools of object-oriented design (Booch, OMT, and OOSE)—even a new hire unfamiliar with UML can learn it fairly quickly, if he or she is already versed in one of its three predecessors.

THE TOWER OF BABULL

Once you've decided what tools to use to *design* your systems, the next thing on the agenda is figuring out what you're going to use to *build* the systems. Believe it or not, there are many more programming languages on earth than there are human languages. Each of them has their own peculiar syntax and grammar. This has as much to do with ego as necessity. While much of what shapes a particular language is its intended use, computer people also just like to have their turf. In fact, often, the choice of which language a programmer uses has more to do with familiarity or working style than suitability for the job. This section attempts to discuss, compare, and contrast some of the more important object-oriented programming languages and environments. To fully understand the differences and advantages between these programming languages, we need to first take a brief look at what programming languages are and how they make the computer do work.

How Computers Work

Despite all of the amazing things computers can do, deep down inside, they are no more intelligent than a blender. Push one button to chop, push another button to puree. That's exactly how computers do the things they do, except the buttons are microscopic and embedded in the chip(s) in the computer's *central processing unit* (the computer's "brain"). Also, instead of transforming strawberries and ice cream into milkshakes, the computer transforms raw data into some more useful form, like a report or a graph or a video game (although, personally I think the world would be a better place if the next generation of personal computers had a milkshake feature).

One way to control all the functions of a particular computer would be to have one switch for *each* function (just like the blender). If switch 1 is on, add two numbers; if switch 2 is on, multiply two numbers; if switch 3 is on, move data from one place to another in memory; and so on. However, the downside of doing it this way is that the more functions a computer has, the more switches it needs to have. This is very expensive and inefficient. The solution is to use combinations of switches (rather than just one switch) to activate each function. If you've ever used a digital watch, you've seen an example of how this works. Suppose we have the latest NOBULLOVA X100 digital watch. It only has two buttons, A and B. But the watch itself has *four* functions: show the time, show the date, show the temperature, and play Beethoven's Fifth symphony. You get the time by doing nothing, the date by pushing button A, the temperature by pushing button B, and Beethoven by pushing buttons A and B *at the same time*. Pushing a particular *combination* of buttons selects a particular function. Similarly, *each operation a computer can perform is represented by a specific combination of ON and OFF switches.*

Because it's not possible for us to flip microscopic switches with our fingers, commands are sent to the central processing unit in the form of electronic signals. Imagine that a given computer chip has been designed to use eight switches (numbered 1 through 8) to represent all of its functions. For example, whenever the computer receives a signal that turns switches 1 through 6 off and switches 7 through 8 on, the computer adds two numbers; or if the computer receives a signal that turns switches 1 and 8 on and switches 2 through 7 off, the computer moves data from one place in memory to another.

As a matter of convenience, programmers often represent a signal that turns a switch on with a "1" and the signal that turns a switch off with a "0". So to continue with the preceding computer chip example, the number 00000011 means "turn switches 1 through 6 off and turn switches 7 through 8 on" and the number 10000001 means "turn switches 1 and 8 on and turn switches 2 through 7 off." Therefore, the number 00000011, in this example, means "add two numbers" and the number 10000001 is the code for "move data from one place in memory to another." Each operation a computer can perform has such a numeric representation or *operation code* (*opcode*).

In the previous example, we said that opcode 00000011 causes the computer to add two numbers. But how does the computer know *which* two numbers to add? Actually, a complete *instruction* for the computer (called a *machine instruction*) includes both the code for the operation to be performed and a reference to the data on which it is to be performed. For example, the complete machine instruction to add two numbers might look something like this: 00000011 11011000. The first part is the opcode for ADD and the second part tells the computer where to find the numbers to add and where to put the result. Yuk! That may be easy for some machine to understand, but what human being wants to look at *that* mess?

Programming Languages

The entire set of instructions that a particular type (e.g. Macintosh, IBM compatible PC, etc.) of computer can perform is called its machine language. Since every kind of computer has different operations it is capable of performing—for example, the big *mainframe* computers that run corporations do things your home computer can't and vice versa—*the machine language (the set of instructions) for each type of computer is different.* Now for the really bad news: A computer program is nothing more than a great big laundry list of machine language instructions, and most computer programs contain thousands or even *millions* of them—no problem for the machine, a trip to the nuthouse for the programmer. Fortunately, that's why somebody back in the dawn of computers created what we now call *high-level programming languages.*

A high-level programming language is a way for human beings to tell a computer what to do using instructions that resemble human written languages or mathematical equations. For example, to add 2 + 2, a C++ programmer might write:

```
Sum = 2 + 2;
```

This is just a wee tad easier to understand than all that 1's and 0's stuff, don't you think? Common high-level languages include COBOL, Fortran, Pascal, C, C++, Smalltalk, Java, BASIC, and so on. Later in this chapter we'll take a peek at a few of them.

After a program is written in a high-level language, it is translated into machine language so the computer can understand it too. There are two primary ways this is done: *compiling* and *interpreting*. A *compiler* is a program that takes files containing high-level language instructions and translates them into machine language. The computer can then execute the resulting program. An interpreter is a program that translates each high-level language instruction one by one into machine language instructions *as the program executes.*

The best way to understand the difference between compilation and interpretation is to think of two people trying to communicate who speak different languages. Imagine one speaks English and the other speaks Japanese. One way the English person could get his point across is to write a letter in English, then have someone translate it into Japanese. This is very efficient since the Japanese person can read the letter in her own language very quickly, without interruption. The problem is that if the English-speaker decides he wants to change something, he has to edit the original letter, give it to the translator again, then forward it to the Japanese person who has to read the whole thing over again.

The other way the English-speaker can communicate with the Japanese-speaker is to hire an interpreter to stand between them. Each sentence the English speaker says will then be translated into Japanese as he says it. The advantage is that the English speaker can now easily revise what he says interactively; the disadvantage is that the transfer of information is a lot slower because the Japanese speaker must wait for each sentence to be translated.

In general, compilers produce programs that run faster because all translation to machine language is done *before* the program begins executing. The disadvantage of compiled programs is that the entire program must be translated into machine language before it can be tested—a process that can take hours in large programs. This can result in huge productivity losses—any time a bug is found or a change is required, the programmer has to edit the program, then endure the recompile. Interpreted programs don't have this problem, because the program can be revised and run interactively. However, interpreted programs run slower because each high-level language instruction has to be translated into machine instructions before the computer can execute it.

There is a third approach that kind of corrects for the deficiencies of both compilation and interpretation while preserving their respective strengths: compilation to an intermediate language. Using an intermediate language is a lot like speaking in a pidgin. A pidgin is a simplified human pseudo-language used for communication between people who speak different languages. Pidgins commonly evolve in areas where there is heavy commerce between people who speak different languages. Suppose our English-speaker in the previous example knew a hundred words in Japanese, and the Japanese-speaker knew about twenty words in English. It may be possible for them to converse quite freely without the use of translated text or an interpreter, using a simplified language that is somewhere between their two languages. The communication would not be as efficient as sending pure Japanese to the Japanese-speaker would, but it could still be good. Compiling programs to intermediate code is loosely analogous to speaking in a pidgin.

Intermediate code is usually some form of pseudo-machine language that can be rapidly translated into real machine language. There are two different ways that intermediate code is used: compile-interpret and incremental compilation. In the compile-interpret approach, the original high-level language instructions are compiled to the intermediate language; the intermediate language is interpreted when the program runs. This gives you a program that runs almost as fast as a pure compiled program, yet can still be edited and tested interactively. Another potential side benefit of this approach is that, as in the case of Java, this little trick can be used to make a compiled program platform-independent (more on that in the section on Java).

In incremental compilation, the high-level language instructions are translated into the intermediate language *as the programmer types in the program*. The intermediate code is then compiled into machine language after the program is finished. The beauty of incremental compilation is that the program has all the performance advantages of a compiled program, but only takes seconds to recompile. This makes interactive testing and editing possible.

Regardless of how the high-level language gets translated to machine language, the selection of a programming language should be regarded like the selection of any other tool: Find the best one for the job you are trying to do. The remainder of this chapter introduces the various types of object-oriented languages and highlights the most widely used language(s) of each type.

OK, so now we know what a high level language is—what makes a language *object-oriented*? An object-oriented programming language is one that has built-in language features for creating classes, inheritance, creating objects, message passing between objects, and polymorphism. While it's possible to *design* a program written in *any* programming language in an object-oriented way, only languages that support the preceding five features are considered to be truly object-oriented.

Hybrid Languages

A hybrid object-oriented language is a traditional program-ming language that has been extended to include some or all of the features that make a language object-oriented. Virtually all of the traditional programming languages, such as COBOL, FORTRAN, PL/I, and C have had at least some of the five basic object-oriented features added to them. For example, C++ is the C programming language plus object-oriented features and some other nice enhancements.

The advantage of hybrids is that it's not such a big stretch for a programmer skilled in the base language to pick up the new syntax for objects. Another advantage is that object-oriented modules can be introduced into legacy applications quite easily. The downside is that, since the hybrid language is just a superset of the base language, the legacy programmer can keep on using the same *non*–object-oriented programming style he or she has always used. In other words, there is no built-in enforcement of object-oriented programming. The result is often, especially on first object-oriented projects, programs that are a mix of objects, structured, and unstructured code. This kind of program is something I refer to as object slop and it's often harder to understand and maintain than the worst struc-tured or even unstructured code in big programs.

Some hybrid languages include the new object-oriented ver-sions of COBOL, FORTRAN, and PL/I. However, hands down, the king of the hybrids is C++.

C++

The C programming language was a systems programming language developed at AT&T Bell Labs specifically for the purpose of writing the Unix operating system. It is a structured programming language that has a lot of very powerful features for doing the kinds of low-level operations that operating system programmers have to do. It became popular with programmers because (1) it and the Unix operating system were initially distributed *free* along with the source code, and (2) it gives the programmer a lot more direct control over the machine than most programming languages do.

In the early 1980s, an AT&T Bell Labs employee named Bjarne Stroustrup, began tinkering with adding object-oriented features into the C language, and somewhere around 1985 the language C++ was released to the world. The name C++ is kind of a programmer's pun: In the C language, the expression "C++;" means, "Add 1 to the number stored in a variable named 'C'." In other words, C++ is "one step beyond" C, which is true. C++ has all of the features of C, plus a whole bunch of new features and the object-oriented extensions.

Advantages of C++:

✪ Very similar to C. The *language* learning curve for experienced C programmers is small—it's learning object-oriented programming that's hard.

✪ Powerful. Allows direct manipulation of system storage and devices.

✪ High-performance, compiled code.

✪ Implements all object-oriented constructs, and even offers multiple inheritance, which none of the other mainstream object-oriented languages do.

✪ C++ compilers are now available on virtually every operating system in existence. Therefore, C++ skills developed for one operating system can be used to write applications on another.

DISADVANTAGES OF C++:

✪ Object model not enforced by C++. Programmers can easily write non–object oriented programs or object slop.

✪ Dangerous. Errant programs can corrupt data or even crash some operating systems.

✪ No garbage collection. It is possible for programmers to forget to destroy objects that are no longer in use. Over time this can exhaust the amount of available memory on the computer.

✪ Unless an incremental compiler is used, compile times can be quite lengthy for large programs. This can slow down development and debugging efforts.

✪ C++ was only recently standardized. Just as there are many dialects of each human language, where there are no standards, dialects of programming languages pop up. Even though C++ is finally standardized now, there are still many subtle, annoying differences in the C++ language depending on what operating system or what vendor's compiler you're writing code for. These discrepancies can hamper efforts to make a single C++ program run on different kinds of systems and affect delivery dates.

WHEN TO USE C++:

C++ is best suited to applications that need to have direct control of system resources. Typical applications include: operating systems programming, database development, system utilities, and scientific applications. It's also ideal for performance-critical applications like transaction processing. It is also used for numerous other applications, like games, word processing programs, and data entry applications. However, there are other object-oriented languages that are safer and easier to program in, like Java, that are actually the better choice for these kinds of applications.

PURE OBJECT-ORIENTED LANGUAGES

Smalltalk and (arguably) Java are examples of "pure" object-oriented languages. Some other pure object-oriented languages include Eiffel and Self. They are *pure* because they were designed from the ground up to be object-oriented. What does that mean?

✪ All entities in a pure object-oriented language are *objects*.

✪ The programming language *forces* the programmer to write programs in an object-oriented way—it is not possible (without a great deal of difficulty) to write a program in these languages in a structured or unstructured way.

✪ The language contains all of the features that define an object-oriented program: classes, objects, message passing, inheritance, and polymorphism.

Smalltalk and Java are the big kids on the block in the pure object-oriented languages category. While the other pure object-oriented languages have lots of good features and are interesting, these two dominate the stage. Therefore, language overviews in this section will be limited to Smalltalk and Java.

SMALLTALK

Smalltalk, considered by many the most technically pure implementation of an object-oriented language, is still the language of choice of many object-oriented extremists. It evolved during the early 1970s out of research at the Xerox Palo Alto Research Center (PARC), led by Alan Kay.

One interesting aspect of Smalltalk is that the language and software that Smalltalk programmers use to develop programs (the *development environment*) is virtually inseparable. The development environment allows the programmer to interactively develop, compile, (to intermediate code), and execute their programs. This greatly increases the speed with which applications can be built.

Another signature feature of Smalltalk is that it is the only mainstream object-oriented language that has true message passing between objects. Both C++ and Java *simulate* message passing by having one object directly execute (*call*) a method on the target object. The net effect is the same: object A gets object B to do something for it; object A waits until object B has finished doing its thing. The difference between the two approaches is largely academic.

ADVANTAGES OF SMALLTALK:

✪ Because the language is compiled to intermediate code, development is much faster than with traditional compiled languages. The advent of incremental compilers for C++ is threatening this advantage, however.

✪ The object implementation is so strong in this language that the programmer is *forced* to write entirely object-oriented code. Even the elements of the Smalltalk language itself are represented as objects.

✪ Because the programmer is forced to program in an object-oriented way, Smalltalk makes an excellent language for teaching people the right way to do object-oriented programming.

✪ Integration of the programming language and the development environment facilitates developing graphical user interface applications. It is possible to see how a program is going to look as you develop it.

✪ Garbage collection is built in. The memory used by an object is guaranteed to be reclaimed when a object is no longer used.

✪ The Smalltalk *virtual machine* concept makes it easy to port a Smalltalk application to platforms other than the one on which the application was developed (virtual machines are explained in the section on Java).

Disadvantages of Smalltalk:

✪ Because of Smalltalk's heavy reliance on its integrated development environment, the language is very much tied to the vendors who produce the development environment. As a result, Smalltalk programs can only be easily ported to systems supported by the *tool vendor* from which you bought your implementation of Smalltalk.

✪ Professional Smalltalk development environments tend to be at least twice the cost of comparable C++ and Java development environments.

✪ Because of the popularity of Java, fewer and fewer universities are offering courses in Smalltalk. But more importantly, fewer students are interested in learning it. To truly get a feel for the situation, go to any computer bookstore and count the number of Java books relative to the number of Smalltalk books (if you can even find one).

One myth that is commonly associated with object-oriented programs, and Smalltalk programs in particular, is that the performance is terrible. This is simply not true. The original Smalltalk versions *were* very slow, but the compilers have matured over time and now Smalltalk programs run about as fast as anything else. The performance characteristics of a particular programming language are determined more by the quality of the compiler or interpreter used than by any inherent qualities of the language itself.

WHEN TO USE SMALLTALK:

A decision to invest in Smalltalk in the late twentieth/early twenty-first century is a questionable one. Smalltalk is best for writing applications that have a graphical user interface, although Smalltalk programs can also run on operating systems that don't have graphical user interfaces. If you have a team that is skilled in the language, it can be used for fairly rapid application and prototype development. However, since Java can do everything Smalltalk can do, is much more widely accepted, and costs a lot less, one has to ask, why bother? Also, Java and component-based application builders, like Visual Basic, while not as elegant, are decidedly stomping the life out of Smalltalk in the GUI application space. Smalltalk's not dead yet, but with Microsoft behind Visual Basic and IBM, Sun Microsystems, Oracle, and basically the rest of the computer industry actively promoting Java, you might consider saving some shelf space near your eight track tapes and home movie film for Smalltalk.

Java

Java is the love child of Sun Microsystems, a Silicon Valley computer manufacturer—and it's a very interesting creature. In typical Silicon Valley style, the group that created Java was given a mission statement that said something like, "Go make something cool." Oddly enough, they did. While billed as a object-oriented programming language, it's really more of a chameleon. Viewed in one light, it's a pretty good object-oriented programming language; viewed in a different light, it's an operating system; viewed in another light, it's a design for a computer chip; and viewed in yet another light, it's an Internet enabling technology. OK, that said, what the heck *is* it? To answer that question, lets take a peek under the hood.

At the highest level, Java is a pure object-oriented programming language. It looks like C++, with none of the disadvantages and almost all of the advantages. In addition, it incorporates the best features of Smalltalk, with none of the disadvantages. Also, a program written in Java only needs to be compiled once, then it can run on almost any kind of computer and operating system. Java programs can even run on Web browsers, credit cards, and household appliances. But how do they *do* that?

Recall from the introduction to this section that every type of computer has its own machine language. For this reason, a program written for one type of machine (e.g. Macintosh, PC, etc.) must be must be recompiled (translated to machine language) for *every other type of computer* on which it is to be used. In addition, it may be necessary to make changes to the program itself to account for differences in the compilers available on each type of machine (this is like the subtle differences you might see in two independent translations of a French poem into English). These kinds of *portability* issues greatly hinder the ability to create programs that can run on all kinds of computers. Smalltalk solved this problem—and Java copied the solution—by using the concept of a *virtual machine*.

Consider the following scenario: The machine code of a PC and a multimillion-dollar IBM mainframe are very different— each has a very different purpose, and consequently, each has a very different set of functions it can perform. The PC can display pretty graphics, but doesn't need to store terabytes of data; the mainframe can't do graphics very well, but can store terabytes of data. Also, the two machine designs were created in two totally different eras. To further complicate things, the machine code for the IBM mainframe was designed by IBM, the machine code for the PC was designed by Intel. As a result, the machine language on a PC is *radically* different than the machine language used on an IBM mainframe. So how do you write a program that you can run on either computer without having to recompile? The solution is to use a *virtual machine*.

A virtual machine is a program that *simulates* a real computer and even has its own machine language. As a result, programs can actually be compiled to run on a virtual machine *instead of a real computer.* Under the covers the virtual machine translates its virtual machine language into the *real* machine language of *each* computer that it runs on. This is what makes the magic of Java happen: The Java virtual machine is now available on virtually every type of computer and operating system there is. Therefore, by compiling Java programs for the Java virtual machine, *programmers don't have to be concerned with what type of computer or operating system their programs will be running on.* The programs will run on virtually every major platform including (but not limited to) Microsoft Windows (3.1, 95, 98, and NT), OS/2, all brands of Unix, Macintosh, VM, OS/400, and MVS.

This "write once, run-anywhere" concept is also what makes Java an ideal language for the Internet. Since the Internet is really nothing more than a jumbled mass of interconnected computers of all types, a program written for use on the Internet must be able to run on any kind of computer. Java is absolutely ideal for this application. The secret is that every major Web browser now contains a Java virtual machine. When you connect to a Web site that uses Java, the Java program (or *applet*) is loaded by your Web browser into the browser's virtual machine and executed. There are growing number of applications for this technology. Some of the more popular ones include on-line loan calculators, interactive "chats," and on-line shopping. As an aside (while we're on the subject of the Internet), you may hear people talk about something called *JavaScript*. JavaScript is *not* Java. JavaScript is a *structured*, mini programming language that vaguely resembles

Java. Java is an *object-oriented*, full-scale programming language. JavaScript is used to create special effects on Web pages, such as alert windows, frames, scrolling text, and so on.

Hey, wait a minute! If all the Java virtual machine does is *simulate* a real computer, why can't someone build a real computer that uses the same machine language (called Java *byte code*) as the Java virtual machine? Then you wouldn't have to simulate anything—Java programs could just run directly on the machine. The answer is: They can and they have (whoever "they" are). In fact, so called "Java chips" can be embedded in anything from credit cards to household appliances to cars. Imagine this: Your traditional credit card gets replaced by a *smart card* that contains a Java chip and a lot of personal information about you. You land in Houston on business and check into the hotel. When the clerk runs your card through, a Java program runs *on the chip inside your credit card* that compares your personal preferences and expense account limits against restaurants and attractions in the area. The clerk is able to hand you a printout with a list of local restaurants tailored to your budget and tastes along with directions. This same technology can be used to make the thermostat in your house smarter, your cell phone more usable, and your car more fuel-efficient.

A final role of Java is as an operating system. An operating system is a special kind of program that manages the resources of your computer. For example, the Microsoft Windows operating system manages your printers, display device, memory, disk drives, and mouse, and loads and executes programs, etc.

While the Java virtual machine can run on Windows, it can also behave like an operating system itself: It manages display devices, memory, loads and executes programs, and so on. So who needs Windows? Exactly.

Java is a big threat to Microsoft, and as a result Microsoft has become a big threat to Java. While openly endorsing the Java programming language, Microsoft has been very actively selling people their own version of Java with extra features not included in the base Java language. The apparent strategy is to get people hooked on using the extensions so that *their applications cannot be ported to other platforms.* If Microsoft succeeds, they will effectively destroy the portability of Java programs and lock people into using Windows. If this happens, Java will become nothing more than a better version of C++. To combat this, Sun Microsystems, IBM, Oracle, and a number of other key players in the software industry have started the 100% Pure Java initiative: a program designed to encourage the industry to use nothing but the core Java language and avoid proprietary extensions. The goal is to prevent Java from becoming tied to any one operating system so its full potential can be realized.

ADVANTAGES OF JAVA:

✪ 100% Pure Java is not tied to any operating system, development environment, or vendor.

✪ Write once, run anywhere, including all major computer systems, the Internet, handheld devices, and smart cards.

✪ Garbage collection is built in. The memory used by an object is guaranteed to be reclaimed when a object is no longer used.

✪ Almost universal computer industry endorsement (with one notable exception).

✪ Easy for C and C++ programmers to learn because Java is derived from C++.

✪ Prevents direct access to the computer's memory, so a malfunctioning program cannot corrupt the system, overwrite data, or crash other programs.

✪ Everything needed to develop Java applications can be obtained for *free* on the Internet from Sun's Javasoft Web site. You can also purchase complete commercial development environments from all the major software tools vendors for *very* reasonable prices. The latter approach is recommended—the tools and the compilers are much better.

✪ Java is very actively taught in almost all colleges and universities now, and there are dozens of books available on the subject.

DISADVANTAGES OF JAVA:

✪ There's a six-hundred-pound gorilla who wants very badly to sit on it.

✪ Invented by a corporation rather than a standards committee—this means that the language has some truly quirky features that were the whim of the project architect.

✪ It is still an immature, relatively new language, and as such, is currently undergoing a lot of changes.

✪ Lacks the power of C++—too far removed from the hardware to be used as a systems programming language (except on machines based on Java chips).

✪ Most of the compilers are still immature—Java applications today don't perform as well as applications written in other object-oriented languages.

WHEN TO USE JAVA:

Java is an incredibly versatile language that can be used for an endless variety of applications. It is best suited to applications that do not have to manipulate the computer's memory directly, and it should be your first choice when portability is of primary consideration. For example, suppose you want the IT department to produce a company-wide phonebook application—type in a name, and up pops the person's internal and external phone numbers, their address, their e-mail address, and a photograph. The engineering staff is all on Unix-based workstations, the administration is on PCs, and the marketing group uses Macintoshes. Java is the ideal choice here, because (assuming the programmer sticks to 100% Pure Java) the application can be written once and distributed to all departments—as is.

If your company has an *intranet*, many Java applications *do not even have to be distributed directly to end users*—everyone can just access them through their Web browsers. The phonebook example given above is a perfect application for this kind of deployment. The best part is that, if you use Web-deployed applications, your IT people no longer have to visit each office to install, configure, or upgrade software. Think how much money that could save. But don't lay them all off yet, there are still plenty of applications that do have to be installed the old fashioned way.

Component-Based Programming

So far in this text we have loosely used the terms object and class interchangeably with the term component. It is now necessary to refine the terms a little bit. For the purposes of this section, let's just say a software component is an *application building block*. Components in a running program can be a single object, contain hundreds of objects, or not have anything to do with objects at all; a component can also be a structured module or even an entire program. A component is simply a subassembly that performs some kind of function in a program. Buttons, scroll bars, spreadsheets, timers, a statistical calculation module, database access functions, and anything you can possibly imagine can be packaged as components. Building programs from ready-made components is the next logical evolution of object-oriented programming.

To build programs from components, programmers draw connections between components on the screen, then specify how they interact. For example, suppose you give your favorite programmer, Bubba, the task of creating a simple program that displays the daily sales total from the Tokyo office when you click a button on the screen of your PC in New York. Bubba begins by "dragging and dropping" a button component, a data access component, and a text field component into his development environment. He then uses the mouse to draw a link from the button component to the data access component. Next, he then indicates that when the button is clicked, the data access component is to retrieve the sum of all the daily sales from the Tokyo sales database. Bubba then uses the mouse to indicate that the data returned by the data access component is to be displayed by the text field component. *That's it!!!* The program is complete and ready to run. That's the magic of component-based programming. Forget writing hundreds of lines of code, forget trying to remember where hundreds of objects are and what they're doing. Just point and click and you're done. Well, OK, it's not quite that simple, but *close.*

So called *visual builders* such as IBM VisualAge (C++ and Smalltalk)[1], and Microsoft Visual Basic, and component-based programming models like Sun Microsystems' JavaBeans all facilitate component-based programming. Both VisualAge (C++ and Smalltalk) and JavaBeans are based on object-oriented concepts; Visual Basic uses a pseudo–object-oriented model. Visual Basic is pseudo–object-oriented because its components *can*, but do not *have* to be built in an object-oriented way. Also, Visual Basic does not support direct inheritance, so one component design cannot be directly used as the basis for another kind of component— this greatly hampers the programmer's ability to reuse code (one of the key benefits of object technology). Since it is impossible to cover the endless variety of products available for component-based programming, we're just going to look at Visual Basic and IBM's VisualAge family of products for contrast. Then we'll wrap up with a peek at JavaBeans.

---

[1]IBM also makes a visual builder for Java. However, since Java components (Java Beans) can be used in any Java development environment (not just VisualAge), discussion of Java component programming is deferred to the later section on Java Beans.

The Visual Basic Approach

In component-based programming, the amount of code that has to be written by the programmer is determined by a programming model employed by the tool, the number of predefined components supplied with the tool, the number of third-party components available, and the programming language supported by the tool. Visual Basic's programming model is based on *events*. In Visual Basic, clicking a button is, for instance, an event. The program logic to respond to *every possible event* in a program must be written manually by the programmer. Visual Basic requires the programmer to write more code by hand than any other popular visual builder. However, this disadvantage is offset somewhat by the fact that Visual Basic gives you a lot more stock components.

There are literally hundreds of components (called ActiveX controls or ActiveX components)—from both Microsoft and countless outside vendors—available for Visual Basic. The result is that while Visual Basic programmers write more code by hand, they need a lot less expertise to do powerful things. Also, Visual Basic programmers are able to create a wide variety of new applications without having to create a lot of new components. This is one of the reasons why Visual Basic is still so hugely popular in corporate IT shops. The big catch is, Visual Basic can only produce programs that run on computers that use the Windows family of operating systems.

ADVANTAGES OF VISUAL BASIC:

✪ Microsoft does an excellent job of encouraging vendors to write companion products for their software. There are literally thousands of ActiveX controls and components available.

✪ The large number of available components reduces the skill level required for programmers.

✪ Visual Basic is a very popular product—it's relatively easy to find people who are skilled at using it.

✪ It's based on the BASIC (Beginners All-purpose Symbolic Instruction Code) programming language. BASIC is *very* easy to learn.

✪ Visual Basic can be used in conjunction with other Microsoft products—for example, Microsoft Excel itself can be a component of a Visual Basic program.

DISADVANTAGES OF VISUAL BASIC:

✪ Requires the user to write a lot of code to sew components together into a graphical user interface application.

✪ Code reuse is greatly hampered by Visual Basic's lack of inheritance.

✪ Poor enforcement of the object model (or any good coding practices) makes Visual Basic programs harder to maintain. The more unskilled the programmer, the worse the program.

✪ Very high-level: Bugs in components may be difficult or impossible for programmers to find. Also, depending on the type of component, the programmer may have the expertise to understand the problem.

✪ Restricts the user to the Windows platforms—if you have a Macintosh or a Unix machine, you're out of luck.

WHEN TO USE VISUAL BASIC:

Visual Basic can only produce applications for Windows. This currently makes it poorly suited for applications that need to run on a wide variety of machines. The other problem with Visual Basic is that because its object model is so weak, it allows undisciplined programmers to create a hideous mix of object-oriented and non-structured slop code. Unless your IT department has tightly controlled coding standards, large applications can become bug-ridden nightmares. These are important issues to consider if scalability or portability are strategic issues for you. Visual Basic is best suited for prototypes and non–mission-critical GUI applications. However, you can also do real stuff with it, too—there are quite a few commercial software products on the market that were built with Visual Basic.

THE VISUALAGE APPROACH

The programming model employed by VisualAge, based on links, is akin to the one Bubba used in the example at the beginning of this section. In VisualAge, the programmer drags and drops the components she wants into her application, then connects them with links. Each link represents a message sent from one object to another. Under the covers, VisualAge automatically generates virtually all of the high-level language instructions for the application. There are VisualAge visual builders for C++ and Smalltalk that support this programming model.

The advantage of having a visual builder based on an object-oriented programming language is that all components can be inherited into new components and extended. Also, the use of real object-oriented languages and extensive code generation makes it harder for the application programmer to introduce bugs.

Advantages of VisualAge:

✪ All components are classes, so they can easily be inherited and extended. Code reuse is fully supported.

✪ Supports standardized, fully object-oriented languages (C++ or Smalltalk).

✪ Non-visual, component-based applications can be generated for use on most IBM platforms (AS/400, OS/2, AIX, and MVS) and Windows.

✪ Highly optimized incremental compilers; interactive development and debugging; high performance.

Disadvantages of VisualAge:

✪ The latest version of the VisualAge environment only supports visual components on Windows platforms (the same limitation as Visual Basic)

✪ Automatically generated code can often be difficult for a programmer to figure out if manual modifications have to be done.

✪ Components are designed for use with IBM visual builder and compilers.

When to use it VisualAge:

The VisualAge-style visual builders are best used in environments where there are very experienced object-oriented programmers who work with either C++ or Smalltalk. The most suitable applications are large Windows applications, commercial software products, and mission critical or performance sensitive applications. This environment can also be used for rapid development of applications that don't need a user interface and will run on multiple systems.

JavaBeans

As with everything else, Sun Microsystems strove to make Java-Beans take on the best qualities of everything and lose the disadvantages. As the name suggests, JavaBeans are created using the Java programming language. A JavaBean is a group of one or more Java classes bundled together into a single, reusable software component. The key advantage of building components from Java classes is that the components will be independent of any operating system, machine, or software vendor's development environment. JavaBeans can be used to build Internet applications and any other type of program that can be done in Java, including programs that run on devices like microwave ovens and smart cards.

Advantages of JavaBeans:

✪ Independent of any operating system or hardware

✪ Not tied to any vendor's development environment—a 100% Pure Java bean written in Inprise's Borland JBuilder can be used to create programs in IBM's Visual-Age for Java and Microsoft's J++ or any other development environment that supports JavaBeans.

✪ JavaBeans applications have all the other advantages of writing programs in 100% Pure Java.

✪ Full inheritance, code reuse, and object-orientation.

✪ The programming model used to build programs with JavaBeans is entirely determined by the tool you use. This allows programmers to pick whatever environment best fits their working style.

Disadvantages of JavaBeans:

✪ The six-hundred-pound gorilla doesn't like JavaBeans either—JavaBeans are a serious threat to their number-one-selling visual builder.

✪ Java compilers are still not as good as they can be—Java-Beans applications can be quite slow.

✪ There still aren't nearly as many commercially available JavaBeans as there are Visual Basic components. Also, many of the JavaBeans that *are* available aren't as polished as the equivalent ActiveX components.

WHEN TO USE JAVABEANS:

Programs constructed from JavaBeans can be used for any application that it makes sense to use Java for. Think of Java-Beans as just being a faster way to program in Java.

LANGUAGES SUMMARY TABLE

	C++	Smalltalk	Java	Visual Basic
Object-orientation	Hybrid	Pure	Pure	Partial
Classes	Yes	Yes	Yes	Yes
Inheritance	Yes	Yes	Yes	No
Multiple Inheritance	Yes	No	No	No
Objects	Yes	Yes	Yes	Yes
Message Passing	Function calls	Yes	Function calls	Procedure calls and Events
Polymorphism	Yes	Yes	Yes	No
Components	Depends on the development environment	Depends on the development environment	JavaBeans	ActiveX
Applications	• Systems programming • database, • high performance • real-time	• GUI applications	• Multiplatform • Internet • devices, • GUI applications	• Prototypes • GUI applications for Microsoft platforms only

SOFTWARE ASSET MANAGEMENT

One of the most common mistakes companies make in valuing software assets is putting the sole focus on complete software systems. Especially with object-oriented systems, the total value of the *parts* can actually be greater than the value of the whole system. A software component embodies your investment in the labor, expertise, and tools used to create that component. The more a component can be reused in new applications, the greater your return on investment. More importantly, if a given class or component is *not* reused when its functionality is needed in a new application, you will end up paying for the cost of the labor, expertise, and tools required to create a new class or component that does exactly the same thing.

We've already talked a great deal about the importance of designing object-oriented software so that its parts *can* be reused. However, the issue that is largely overlooked by most companies and the software industry as a whole is the *management* of classes and components after they have been created. Here's the problem: It doesn't take long for a company or even a small workgroup to amass a collection of dozens of classes. The collection (or class library) quickly grows so large that no one person is familiar with all the classes in the library. As a result, useful software components are frequently forgotten outside of the context of the first application in which they were used. The problem is further compounded when there are multiple software development groups within a company. How can you know to reuse something if you don't know it exists? The net result is that, without software resource management, you end up paying for the same software to be written over and over again. So what was the point of spending all that money on object technology in the first place?

To realize the benefits of having an inventory of thousands of reusable parts, there has to be some kind of system for cataloging and retrieving those parts—a company's software component assets should be protected and tracked just like any other assets. This really is nothing more than an inventory control problem. The better the system you have for tracking your inventory of software components, the more reuse of them you will get, and the greater your return on investment will be. When determining what tools to purchase to support object-oriented development, some time should also be devoted to developing a system for publishing (within the company) and tracking software components.

An organization's inventory usually consists of class libraries and components developed in-house as well as components and classes purchased from third-party vendors. Components purchased from outside vendors should also be inventoried and cataloged along with the components you develop in-house. As we showed in the last chapter, buying specialized class libraries can be a lot cheaper than hiring programmers to develop the same thing. Therefore, reusing third party components will bring an even greater return than reusing the stuff you develop in-house.

Suppose you're in the financial services business: Group X uses a class library purchased from an outside vendor for doing statistical analysis. Would you really want to pay for some other Group Y to hire a contract programmer with expertise in statistics when everything they need is already in-house? It happens all the time, and it's the sort of thing no one catches. At the line level, the manager of the Group Y has no idea that the first group owns such a class library; at the executive level, you only see a requisition for another contract programmer, and it seems like a reasonable request. A more subtle but equally expensive variation on the theme is that a programmer in group Y is designing and coding virtually the same component a developer in group X did five months ago. So how do you catch stuff like this?

The solution is to make whatever system you have for cataloging software components company-wide. It also needs to be mandatory that everyone use components from this library whenever possible. It's a nice theory, but extremely hard to do in practice. There will be a lot of political, technical, and licensing reasons why many components can't be reused across all groups. However, think of it like basketball: It's a points game. The more reuse you get, the better your return on investment, so any is better than none. Object-oriented techniques facilitate reuse, but it's your responsibility to make it happen.

8 RIDIN' THE HERD

(MANAGING FOR OBJECT TECHNOLOGY)

Hoo doggy, do you have your work cut out for you, partner! Wranglin' object technology projects presents some special challenges for a management team accustomed to traditional software development processes. Projects can't be estimated effectively using the metrics that you've always used. There are all kinds of hidden costs. The development life cycle looks nothing like what you're used to, and the techniques and words are all different. Nonetheless, after you have the right people, skills, and tools, the rest just comes down to good planning and project management. Just do what you do best and you'll have object technology roped and tied in no time.

HAVING A VISION

The first step in any journey is to have some idea where you're going. Object technology should be treated like any other strategic investment: Develop a clear vision for how object technology will be used in your organization. But how do you do that when you are dealing with a technology you've never seen before? Let the company's goals drive your decisions. Some typical goals might be the following:

✪ Reduce manufacturing costs by 25 percent by partnering with a vendor.

✪ Penetrate a new market segment within the next six months.

✪ Grow 50 percent through mergers and acquisitions over the next three years.

✪ Enter a new line of business within the next eighteen months.

✪ Increase revenues by 10 percent through a new technology (e.g., Internet).

✪ Cut expenses by 10 percent for the next two quarters to offset losses in the first half of the year.

✪ Reduce IT cost over the next five years by 40 percent

The way that you would introduce object technology to support each of these goals is very different. For example, to reduce your IT costs over the next five years, you might invest heavily for the next two years in reengineering. If you decided that object technology was the best way to do that, you might retrain some of your existing staff (leaving the rest to maintain the legacy systems while the reengineering effort is underway) and hire some new people specifically skilled in object technology. On the other hand, if your goal is simply to increase the short-term bottom line, you might want to defer any investment in object technology—object technology is an investment in long-term savings. If your goal is to increase revenues through new technologies, you might want to start an entirely new group, staffed with nothing but new hires trained in object technology.

MANAGING CHANGE

Technology is easy; *people* are hard. Once you have a clear idea of how you want to use object technology, the next and most difficult task is introducing it into your organization. Unless you are secretly forming a new group, completely disconnected from everyone else, you will be managing change on some level. If you want to be successful with object technology, it is critical that you realize that what you are asking your existing people to do is much more than just try out a new gizmo. You are asking them to unlearn everything they know about writing software, speak a new language, *program* in a new language, take on new team members, and basically adopt an entirely new culture. Do you think that perhaps they might have a little issue with that?

More so than with any other kind of technology I can think of, if your existing people don't buy into object technology and *understand* it, you might as well not even bother. Programmers who use an object-oriented programming language and continue to program in a non-object-oriented way can absolutely destroy object-oriented software projects. More importantly, they can use the resulting bug-ridden mess to say to you, "See, I told you that object-oriented junk isn't one bit better than what we've already got. Honestly, I don't even know why we're foolin' with it." As a result you might be convinced to throw out the technology rather than look at what the real source of the problem is.

FEAR AND LOATHING IN THE IT DEPARTMENT

The biggest obstacle you have to overcome is *fear*. Programming is a very odd profession—it's the only one where you get to define your own reality. Once a programmer has mastered a particular language, the programmer can make the computer do pretty much anything he or she wants it to do. Where else in your life do you have that kind of control over *anything*? Not surprisingly, all programmers develop a little bit of a god complex. Whenever you introduce a new programming language or environment, you threaten to take away the keys to the universe. The programmer is confronted with no longer being the absolute master of the machine, and as result, losing the self-esteem (read: HUGE ego) that comes with competency. Consequentially, the usual reaction of the programmer to anything new is disdainful rejection. However, if the programmer discovers the technology him or herself, the reaction is just the opposite.

The other kind of fear you have to deal with is the very real (and perhaps justified) fear of replacement or displacement. This will be especially true if you begin to introduce a large number of new faces to help you get started with object technology. Job security fears are one of the most important to deal with, especially if you have a lot of mission-critical legacy systems. You don't want everybody quitting on you and leaving you with systems that none of the new people have a prayer of figuring out. There will be an element of jealousy as well. ("The new kids get to play with all the fun stuff. No fair!")

One way to dispel fears is to provide lots of information. General information about object technology and clear communication of benefits both to the company and the staff (more marketable skills, reduction in effort to develop software, etc.). Similarly, the best way to deal with competency fears is generous distribution of information. Heck, you might even consider passing around a few copies of this book (hint hint hint)—most of the books on object technology are just plain unreadable, even by experienced programmers. However, the best form of information for the folks on the front lines is *training*.

ACHIEVING BUY-IN

As with anything new, it will be a lot easier to get people to accept object technology if they have a big part in bringing it into the company. The more opportunities programmers are given to discover object technology for themselves, the more likely they are to adopt it. Perhaps even take the approach of, "Say Barbara, I read this really good book on object technology over the weekend. Sounds pretty interesting. Think you could do a little research for me and see where we can fit it in?"

The most important thing to remember in achieving buy-in is to avoid managing on high. ("You'll use object technology because I say so and like it!") Involve your people as much as possible in the decision, and listen carefully to objections as they come up (and oh boy, will they ever come up!). A common comment you'll hear from old-school programmers when they first see object-oriented programming is, "There's nothing new here—they just took the same old stuff and put a bunch of fancy new terms on it. I don't see the point in spending the money for this!" Don't be swayed by comments like these. Object technology is *not* a new invention, but it *is* an extension of what has always been done by good programmers. It looks similar, but works very differently. Many old-school programmers just have to *try* a little object-oriented programming before they get it.

The final factor that is crucial to achieving buy-in is having a champion. Actually, there really needs to be two: an executive-level champion and a respected technical champion. The first job of the executive champion should be to hunt down and recruit the technical champion. Where you as the executive can win support by stating it as a strategic direction, throwing money at the problem, and if all else fails, by pure coercion, the technical champion can win support solely on the basis of his or her respect within the IT community. The best thing the executive champion can do is show 100 percent commitment. Be an outspoken advocate and put your money where your mouth is. Don't do it half way. It is very important your people see you are very serious and this is not the latest management fad—this is a permanent change in the way software is developed at your company. Believe me, once people realize how much time and effort it will save them to program this way, they will never want to switch back.

PUTTING ROUND PEGS IN SQUARE HOLES

OK, so now everybody's all fired up about object technology. The next big challenge is integrating it into your culture, and that isn't going to be easy either. There are new people to merge into old teams, there is new software that may have to interact with your old systems, and the IT department may need to adopt a major philosophical shift in the way they deal with customers (both internal and external).

As mentioned in Chapter 6, adoption of the *people* who are experts in object technology is at least, if not more, important than the adoption of the technology. You may have a lot of resistance to begin with, but if the person(s) brought in to help are not liked or respected, an uphill battle will quickly become a losing battle. Even if the team *does* accept the technology, if they don't accept the expert, the first few object-oriented projects will probably be a disaster. Because of code reuse, these disasters will be something that will continue to haunt you for many future projects to come. Unfortunately, at the executive level, you may not fully realize the extent of the problem until down the road, when you see no gains, and probably losses, in productivity for your investment in object technology. Team ownership of the new people is as important as team ownership of the new technology. No one should be hired that isn't approved by the team, regardless of what they know.

Similarly, the biggest *technical* challenge will be how to make your legacy software systems work with the new object-oriented systems. Obviously, all this fancy new object stuff isn't going to buy you much if it can only be used for toy applications. Eventually, the rubber has to meet the road well traveled. Most companies have decades worth of COBOL programs upon which the business depends. Unless you plan to bet the farm and reengineer everything at once (something most people in their right mind would not even *think* of doing), the new object-oriented code has to be designed to talk to the legacy stuff and vise versa. Making this happen will require a high degree of collaboration between the existing staff and the new people skilled in object technology.

One last major change your IT department will have to undergo is a shift in philosophy. Many IT shops are more dictatorships than democracies: They take on a mission, work on the solution in the glass tower, then impose it on the peasants when they're done. This mindset is flat-out not going to work in the object-oriented world. Remember, the key to getting optimal reuse is good design; the key to good design is identifying the right components to build or buy. The key to doing that is *understanding* the business that the software is being created for.

Since the objects in an object-oriented program correspond directly to things in the real world, it is critical that programmers understand the real world they are modeling. If the view of the world is flawed, the system will not contain the right components. Since most business systems model the same basic objects over and over again (customers, products, etc.), poor modeling on one system will impact any other system the components are used to build. The solution is to train your programmers to be better market researchers. The customer, whether internal or external, needs to be continually involved in the development process from the project's inception to rollout. This will be a major shift for a lot of IT people.

One way to encourage a more customer-driven focus is to tie compensation to customer satisfaction. Surveys or product feedback can be used as the measurements of performance; however, this is not enough. Most programmers, especially ones who have been in the game for a long time, have little or no training in interviewing or surveying people. It's not even in their vocabulary. In addition to training your IT staff in object technology, it might be worth it to invest in more touchy-feely classes like "Effective Listening" or "Requirements Gathering" or even "Marketing Research".

PICKING PROJECTS

The key to long-term success with object technology is to start small. The best candidates for early object-oriented projects are small, non–mission-critical applications, like in-house tools and utilities. This will give your programmers a chance to cut their teeth without chewing up anything you really care about. Later, after you have built up an inventory of components and skill in object-oriented analysis, design, and implementation, then you will be ready to fry the bigger fish.

The next type of project that makes sense to tackle is a large-scale, non–mission-critical application or new technology. Company-wide applications that are used for non-critical information dissemination, such as on-line phonebooks or Internet applications, are ideal candidates.

Only after accumulating a significant amount of technical talent, skill, and experience in object technology should you venture into mission critical applications—regardless of whether you are developing them from the ground up or reengineering significant legacy systems. This kind of development is always a bet-the-business kind of decision and should be handled with the utmost care—especially, reengineering.

Reengineering is pretty strenuous stuff—no matter what kind of programming techniques you use. Good candidates for reengineering are programs that have a long history of bugs or contain notoriously bad code that no one really understands. This kind of code will eventually become a liability, if it's not already (as most of us discovered with the Year 2000 Problem). However, once your team has become proficient in object technology, anything's fair game.

PLANNING PROJECTS

The secret to the success of any project is good planning, whether you are building an addition on your house or a multimillion-dollar software system. There is no technology in the world that will relieve you of the need to be a good planner, and object technology is no exception. In a lot of ways, it will require you to be a better planner of software projects than you ever were before. This section does not attempt to be a comprehensive guide to object-oriented project planning— there are entire books written on the subject of software project planning—this is simply a quick introduction to the important issues.

To plan for object technology effectively, you not only need a detailed plan for the current project, but also a good idea of subsequent projects as well. A good object-oriented architect is as much a psychic as a designer of software systems. To get optimal reuse, when the architect designs or purchases components for the current project, he or she must have in mind what they might be used for in future projects. The more information you can supply to your systems architects about what projects you plan to do later, the better job they can do of designing the current project. This why having a vision of the future is so critical.

The toughest aspect of planning for object-oriented projects is dealing with the uncertainty introduced by iterative development (the way object-oriented projects are built up through numerous cycles of design, implementation, and review rather than the more tradition design everything, implement everything, then fix it approach used in traditional development). How can you know how long something is going to take or how big the effort is going to be if the design keeps changing? Well, it's really not quite that wild and woolly. First of all, you should still have a formal specification of *what* the overall system is supposed to do; this should be sufficient to give you a rough-cut estimate of the size of thing you are trying to build. Also, you decide in advance how many iterations you want to go through before final deployment. A single iteration is a sort of mini-project in and of itself, with its own milestones and deliverables. Each iteration just adds a portion of the total function required for the system.

SIZE THE EFFORT

After you've determined what functionality is going to be in the system, you need to get your arms around just how big the effort is going to be. This can be gathered from a gut-feel estimate by the architect, or you can attempt to get a more scientific estimate by soliciting a lower-level estimate from each implementer. When your team is new to object technology, plan on these estimates being *wildly* wrong. Especially on the first few projects when you are just beginning to build up your inventory of components and skills, everything is going to take much longer than you expect it to. Build in a *lot* of padding to your estimates; identify high-risk items and have contingency plans in place for each of them. After you have a good library of components to draw from, you will begin to see the return on investment in object technology, and projects will begin to take less time.

The two most common measures for evaluating the size of a software project are *source lines of code* (SLOC or just LOC) and *Function Point Analysis* (FPA). Both of these have problems when used for sizing object-oriented development projects. The SLOC approach is the most intuitive. It attempts to measure the size of a software development by the number of high-level language instructions that programmers will have to write (the estimate is based on the assumption that one typed line of text in a program is roughly equivalent to one instruction). Based on the estimated number of lines of source code, you can look at historical data to estimate the amount of time and resource required (and consequently, cost) of developing each line of code. This estimating technique has a lot of holes in it, but it can be used to give you a rough idea of size for traditional programming efforts. However, there are several problems when it is applied to object-oriented software development— some short-term, some permanent.

One of the key problems is when your team takes on its first few object-oriented development projects, each line of code will take longer (on average) and be more expensive than what your historical data reflects. Using SLOC measures on your first couple of object-oriented projects will result in estimates that can be wildly low. However, as you begin to build up an inventory of components and skill in object-oriented programming, things will swing in the other direction. A lot fewer lines of code will be required to build very big things, and each line of code written will take a lot less work (it's a lot easier to write code that utilizes existing components than to write the classes to *create* the components). So once again, your historical data may serve to trip you up; estimates may end up being grossly conservative. This can cause you to overstaff, water down, or throw out perfectly good projects.

The more permanent problems with SLOC center around iterative development. Since the implementation details are fuzzier in the beginning of object-oriented projects than with tradition development, it's a lot harder to get a feeling for how many lines of code will have to be written. It is only after several iterations of actually *writing code* that you finally begin to get an idea of how much code will have to be written. By then, it's too late to estimate. Also, lines-of-code estimates are only as reliable as your programmers' guesses as to how much code they will have to write. If your team is new to object-oriented programming, then they will have no idea what they're in for. No guess will even come close. However, if you hire experienced object-oriented architects or if your existing team builds up a little experience in object-oriented programming, it will become possible for them to give fairly credible estimates based on SLOC.

Function Point Analysis is becoming increasingly popular because it looks and feels more scientific than SLOC. More importantly, it is based on a system of estimation that is not tied to the design or implementation of the software system; it is derived solely from the description of what the system is supposed to do (its *functional* specification). Each thing that the system is supposed to do is categorized by whether it involves external inputs (e.g., data coming in from tape or disk), external outputs (e.g., printed reports), queries (e.g., users submitting online forms and waiting for a result), external interfaces (e.g., system A gets data from system B), and internal "files" (e.g., the accounts receivable subsystem transfers a bunch of information to the billing subsystem). Each function that the system is to perform is given a score based on its category and estimated complexity. All the scores are added up, and the sum is multiplied by a factor (between .65 and 1.35) that is supposed to account for the overall complexity of the system and the environment in which it operates. The resulting number is the function point score.

The final step is to convert function points into lines of code. What?!? That's right, FPA is just a supposedly more *consistent* way of estimating lines of code (although some companies also use FPA as a measure of productivity). The whole idea is so Joe and Betty Sue can look at the same project and get a some-where-in-the-same-ballpark-number lines of code estimate. For each programming language, there are people who have figured out an *average* number of lines of code that correspond to one function point. You can also do your own averages based on in-house statistics. For example, if you determine that, on average, one function point takes 110 lines of COBOL code to implement, a 2000 function-point program will require 220,000 lines of code. From this information an experienced estimator can get an idea of how long the project is going to take and how much it's going to cost.

FPA has its share of detractors. Criticisms include the following:

- ✪ Estimates are still dependent on the technology used to implement the system.

- ✪ It's based on the assumption that every software system works like a transaction-oriented business system.

❂ It's about as genuinely scientific as phrenology. There can be wide variations in estimates between individuals, and its statistical foundations are shaky at best.

❂ The data supporting its ability to measure program functionality is weak.

❂ It still relies to a great deal on subjective estimates.

❂ It's ridiculously complicated for the quality of the estimates it provides.

The only point I don't totally agree with is the one about it being dependent on technology (in other words, the programming language used to implement the system). I can tell you from personal experience, it takes a heck of a lot longer to write a program in some languages than others. The programming language C, for example, is a very powerful language, but the trade-off is that the programmer has to write a lot of lines of code to get the machine to do fairly simple things. BASIC, on the other hand, isn't as powerful, but it lets you do simple things with very simple commands. Is factoring in the technology used really such a bad thing? For example, compare a program that does nothing but print "NO BULL" to the screen written in C to the same program written in BASIC:

C Program	BASIC Program

```#include <stdio.h>```
```main()```
```{```
``` printf ("NO BULL\n");```
```}```
	```PRINT "NO BULL"```

FPA really falls apart in estimating object-oriented lines of code because its functionality weighting system has no provision for using components rather than writing code. For example, suppose a proposed system requires some data to be extracted from a database, then passed to another part of the system, which stores the data in a new database. Conventional FPA would estimate this feature to cost a lot of function points to implement. However, if all the database access functionality is built from reusable database components, the actual number of lines of source code written might only be two or three. In fact, the more reuse, the worse a conventional FPA estimate will be. Conversely, on early projects, FPA will tend to estimate the work too low, because there will not be a lot of reuse and because a lot of extra effort will have to be expended creating components. There is no provision in the FPA model for the cost of creating reusable components.

Numerous "scientific" methods of estimating object-oriented software size have been proposed, but so far none have really caught on. Even the FPA method has been enhanced to deal with object-oriented projects. There is no silver bullet yet, however; people are still working on the problem, and a solution is desperately needed. With the size of software systems growing and growing, the current margins of error are becoming less and less acceptable. By traditional programming standards, when you got an estimate that was only off by 10 percent, you were thrilled—big programs used to be 50,000 to 100,000 lines of code. Today, 1,000,000 lines of code and up are becoming increasingly common, especially in commercial software applications. Can you really afford to have estimates that are off by 100,000 lines of code (10 percent of 1,000,000)? This is a trend that will continue as memory and disk prices continue to fall and user interfaces and applications become increasingly more sophisticated.

Whatever estimating technique you use, generously pad estimates on early object-oriented projects, but view estimates of later projects as conservative. Also, regardless of whether you use object technology or not, use a mix of intuition and formal estimating tools. If a number doesn't look right to you, trust your instincts. The most important thing to remember is that early object-oriented projects require more bodies, take longer, and have a bigger learning curve than you're used to. However, if you've done everything right, later projects will surprise you with how fast and how inexpensively they come in.

DIVVYING UP THE CHIPS

Once the architect or project manager has a clear vision of *what* needs to be done, he or she can begin to divide the project up into its fundamental tasks. In object-oriented projects, development assignments are organized by both classes and system functions (line items). For example, Jerry may be responsible for implementing the system function that takes customer orders. As a result, he needs to implement a **Customer** class. This class might also be used by Buffy who is building the part of the system that handles billing. The additional components she implements are **Invoice** and **Account**. In object-oriented development, "work" should not only be delegated to people, but also to libraries of reusable components. Decomposition of the project into tasks should include an appraisal of what pieces of the system can simply be *purchased* in the form of frameworks, class libraries, or components from outside vendors or reused from the company's existing class libraries.

MEASURING SUCCESS

Everything's in place now, and you've done an excellent job of change management and planning. How do you determine if it was all worth it? One of the toughest things about valuing object technology is determining its benefit early on. Since your first project (and possibly the second as well) may take *longer* (depending on how much code you buy versus how much you build) than traditional projects, it can be very difficult to measure what object technology is buying you in the short term. It may take a real leap of faith to stay with object technology for the long haul. But don't let the expectation of inefficiencies blind you to *excessive* inefficiency. In fact, if anything you should be more sensitive to it, especially if you have taken the option of converting your existing crew into object-oriented programmers. *Caveat emptor*.

The first step is to develop a base line of measurements using what you already know about your current software development practices. Calculate conventional things like cost per line of code, and average implementation times. Track defects and the rate at which defects get resolved. How long does it take to adapt the system? You might also want to measure intangibles like customer (internal or external) satisfaction. Once you have a baseline in place, you are in a better position to compare *results*.

The baseline is your object technology reality check. What is the average cost per line of code to develop software? While reuse may make it necessary to write *less* code, what is the cost of the code you did write? How long does it typically take to implement particular kinds of functions? Effectively measuring these results can be as challenging as estimating them for object-oriented software. When you estimate the costs of developing object-oriented software, it's very important to remember to include the cost of purchasing or licensing class libraries, frameworks, or components from outside vendors.

Defect rates and defect resolution turnaround times are metrics that are fairly easy to track. If you keep statistics on these kinds of things, it will be easy for you to see whether there are more or less problems reported with the object-oriented systems. But here once again, you have to look at the average behavior over the long term. Any new software system is going to have its share of bugs, no matter how it's written—although, if you have the statistics available, it would be very informative to compare the number of defects in your new object-oriented system to the number of defects found when your legacy systems were first deployed. The object-oriented system should come out ahead by far. For example, I have seen projects where object-oriented programming techniques eliminated entire categories of bugs. That doesn't mean that the systems were bug-*free*, but they *were* of much higher quality than the equivalent traditional systems.

One last thing to pay attention to is the success of the business itself—after all, isn't that the ultimate goal of any company? Unfortunately, this is probably the hardest thing to link back to object technology—there are countless other factors both internal and external to the company. While it's virtually impossible to correlate the bottom line directly with your investment in object technology, you *can* get some clues by asking questions like: Has object technology enabled us to adapt our systems more rapidly to changing market conditions? Has object technology given us the ability to deploy new systems faster? Have customers noticed an improvement in service? . . . and so on.

You haven't reached the level you have in your career by accident. Object technology isn't some exotic creature that's beyond your means to manage. It's just another bonbon on life's endless conveyor belt of technological advances. Just rely on the skills, intuition, and experience that have carried you this far, and you should be just fine.

THE TAIL END

Well partners, at short last we've come to the tail end, and that's just the beginning. You now have all the basic information necessary to make intelligent decisions about investing in object technology. It's up to you to make this information work for you. Most of you will get saddle sore your first time out. A few will even get bucked. However, in the long haul, object technology will make your ride a lot smoother. Here are the important things to remember along the way:

- ✪ Using object technology to build software is like building anything else from stock components—it's faster and less expensive. The expensive part is designing the components and making the molds that make the components.

- ✪ Object technology, when used correctly, enables you to leverage your specialists, reduce software costs, shorten development time, and produce software with fewer bugs. The key phrase, however, is: *when used correctly*.

✪ Making the move to object technology is expensive. Don't do it just to be doing it; have a need—and if you do do it, don't do it half way. Invest in the right training, tools, and people.

✪ Hire people with a proven record of *OO success*, not just a lot of experience writing software.

✪ The best way to avoid getting ripped off in a foreign country is to speak the language and know the currency. Use the glossary at the end of this book.

✪ You're not in Kansas any more. Rethink everything you know about estimating software cost and time.

✪ Don't forget, *NO BULL Object Technology for Executives* makes a lovely gift for weddings, birthdays, anniversaries, and many other festive occasions!

Happy trails!

GLOSSARY

abstraction
A representation of a thing that contains just enough of the thing's attributes and behaviors to represent it accurately for a given purpose. For example, a cartoon picture of a cat is an abstraction of a cat; it looks like a cat, but doesn't have fur or leave dead birds on your welcome mat.

attribute
A characteristic common to all objects of a certain class. For example, all objects of the class **Customer** have a *first name*. Attributes may also be called data members, member data, instance data, or members.

applet
A small application program that runs under the control of another program such as a Web browser.

base or **base class**
A class from which another class has inherited. The **Animal** class is the base class for the **Dog** class.

BASIC
Beginner's All-purpose Symbolic Instruction Code. A simple programming language designed for teaching students the basics of computer programming.

behavior
1) the set of all actions a class of objects can perform. "While I sip martinis, Jim will take notes on the behavior of the wildebeest." 2) a specific action that can be performed by all objects of a certain class. For instance, all objects of the **Customer** class can purchase merchandise, return merchandise, or use a coupon. The behaviors of an object can also be called its methods or member functions.

business objects
A library of classes of objects commonly found in business, such as customers, employees, accounts, transactions, etc.

byte code
The pseudo-machine language of the Java virtual machine.

C
A powerful, structured programming language characterized by terse syntax and powerful capabilities for directly manipulating storage.

CASE tools
Computer Aided Software Engineering. Programs that software developers use to graphically represent systems and sometimes even generate source code.

class library
A collection of classes, which were either developed in-house, purchased from outside vendors, or both.

class
The software equivalent of mechanical molds. Just as mechanical molds are used to create parts for mechanical systems, classes are used to create parts (objects) for software systems.

code
Instructions written by computer programmers that tell a computer what to do.

compiler
A computer program that translates programs written by human programmers into the machine language of a given type of computer.

component-based programming
Programming by assembling an application from standard software parts. This usually refers to programming with a visual builder, but can also be used as a synonym for object-oriented programming.

C++
A hybrid object-oriented programming language derived from the C programming language.

data-hiding
The ability of a class of objects to restrict or deny access to its data (attributes) by objects of other classes.

data members
The attributes of an object.

development environment
A collection of tools used to create software.

distributed objects
Objects in one program whose methods can be invoked by objects in another program which may or may not reside on the same machine or even be written in the same programming language.

encapsulation
Hiding an object's internal data and procedures from other objects. Outside objects can only interact with the object through its visible, external behaviors and attributes. For example, a light switch *encapsulates* the electrical circuit it completes. The mechanism of the switch and the wiring that connects it to the light and to the power source are hidden from you. To turn a light on or off, you just flip the switch.

FPA

Function Point Analysis. A method of estimating the amount of effort required to produce a software system based on the system requirements rather than its design or implementation. The result of this kind of analysis is a unit called a function point. Function point estimates can be converted to lines of code estimates once you know what programming language you're going to use.

framework

A group of classes that, together, perform a specific function. Frameworks are analogous to the concept of subassemblies in manufacturing.

function

A type of procedure that is capable of returning a value.

inheritance

The creation of a new class from some other class. The new class contains all of the attributes and behaviors of the parent as well as some new ones of its own.

instance

A particular object of a given class.

instance variable

An attribute of a class that holds data specific to each instance (object) created from the class. For example, a class representing customers might contain an attribute called *name*. Each customer object created from the class will have its own value for the *name* attribute.

instantiation

The creation of an object from a certain class.

interface

The behaviors of objects (of a given class) that are directly accessible by other objects. The rules for how a programmer can use a given software component.

iterative software development life cycle
The software development process most commonly used in the creation of object-oriented software. It consists of the same four basic phases as the waterfall software development life cycle, except that all four phases are repeated, refining the program in stages (a process called *stepwise refinement*), until the project is complete.

JavaScript
A procedural mini-language with Java-like syntax used to make Web pages more interesting. Not to be confused with Java applets, which are programs that run under the control of Web browsers.

Java
A pure object-oriented programming language that borrows the best qualities of both C++ and Smalltalk, while losing most of the bad qualities. Its most significant feature is the ability to run on any kind of computing device, including handheld computers, appliances, and smart cards. This makes the language ideally suited for the Internet.

legacy system
An existing system. Typically this term refers to old mainframe programs; the term also applies to any software system you're stuck with because it's too important to get rid of.

lines of code
One line of code is roughly equivalent to one high-level computer programming language instruction. Lines of code are frequently used to estimate the cost of producing software in structured and unstructured programs.

mainframe
A large-scale computer system that is capable of handling hundreds or even thousands of users and massive amounts of data.

member data or **members**
The attributes of a class of objects.

message
A signal sent from one object to another that causes the target object to perform some behavior.

message passing
When one object signals another object to do something.

methods or **member functions**
Procedures used to manipulate and access the member data of the class of objects to which they belong.

module
A self-contained functional unit of a program. If a program only has one module, the terms module and program are synonymous.

object
The building block of an object-oriented program. Objects are analogous to interchangeable parts used in manufacturing. Just as mechanical devices can be created by bolting parts together, object-oriented programs can be assembled by "bolting" objects together.

object database
A database that represents data in the form of objects. The objects stored in the database are mirror images (stored on a disk drive) of object instances created by a given object-oriented program. Objects that are mirrored in an object database are referred to as *persistent objects*.

object-oriented
Centered around objects or software "parts." An object-oriented program is one that is composed of objects; object-oriented design is software design which is centered around designing the objects that will make up a program; object-oriented analysis is an assessment of a given physical system to determine which objects in the *real* world need to be represented as objects in a given software system.

object technology
The tools, techniques, languages, and processes involved in the production of object-oriented software; the creation of software from reusable parts.

parent or parent class
The same as a base class.

pattern
A named design that solves a particular type of programming problem.

polymorphism
The ability of objects from different classes (all derived from the same base class) to perform a specific behavior differently. A customer, a preferred customer, and a delinquent customer all have a "purchase" behavior, but what happens when instances of each of these classes try to make a purchase may be quite different.

procedure
A group of programming language instructions that perform a specific function. For example, a procedure to "debit-account" might contain instructions that tell the computer to subtract the amount of a debit from a given checking account balance.

relational database
A database in which data appears to users to be stored in tables (rows and columns).

reusable code
Software entities that can be taken from one area of a program and then reused in different areas of the same program or in an entirely different program. For example, the same code that debits accounts in a checkbook program can also be used to debit asset accounts in a general ledger program. If the checkbook and general ledger programs were object-oriented, then the class used in the checkbook program to create account objects could also be used to create account objects in the general ledger program.

SLOC
Source Lines of Code. An estimate of the number of source code program-mers will have to write to implement a software system. Useful for getting a ballpark idea of how big an effort a system is going to be.

Smalltalk
Arguably the most pure object-oriented programming language. Its key features are an integrated development environment and a virtual machine concept. The virtual machine allows Smalltalk programs to be compiled once, then run on multiple platforms. It is also the only popular object-oriented programming language that supports true message passing.

step-wise refinement
See iterative software development life cycle.

subclass
A class created from some other class (its base or parent class).

UML
Unified Modeling Language. A system of diagrams used for modeling object-oriented systems. UML is derived from the Booch, OMT, and OOSE methods of software engineering.

use case
A technique invented by Ivar Jacobson for describing the behavior of a system from an actor's point of view. An actor is a human or machine user of the system. A use case names a *thing* the system can do and shows the way an actor triggers it.

virtual machine
A program that acts like a computer. A virtual machine has its own machine language, which it in turn translates into the machine language of the real computer on which it runs. Programs compiled for a virtual machine can be executed on any type of computer that has a version of the virtual machine, *without recompiling*. Java and Smalltalk both use virtual machines.

visual builder
A program that allows programmers to develop applications by visually arranging and connecting software components on the screen.

waterfall software development life cycle
A software development process in which there are four sequential steps: analyze, design, implement, and test. Some authors insert a fifth step, feedback, at the end.

REFERENCES

Arnold, Ken, and James Gosling. *The Java Programming Language, 2nd ed.* Reading, MA: Addison-Wesley, 1998.

Bar-David, Tsvi. "Object-Oriented Librarianship", *OOPS Messenger.* ACM Press, pp. 1–5, Vol. 5, No. 1, January 1994.

Booch, Grady. *Object Oriented Design with Applications.* Redwood City, CA: The Benjamin/Cummings Publishing Company, Inc., 1991.

Chase, Richard B., and Nicholas J. Acquilano. *Production and Operations Management: A Life Cycle Approach*, 5th ed. Homewood, IL: Irwin, 1989.

Gamma, Erich, Richard Helm, Ralph Johnson, and John Vlissides. *Design Patterns: Elements of Reusable Object-Oriented Software.* Reading, MA: Addison-Wesley Publishing Company, Inc., 1995.

Gray, Jerry L. and Frederick A. Starke. *Organizational Behavior: Concepts and Applications*, 4th ed. Columbus: Merrill Publishing Company, 1988.

Holzner, Steven. *Visual Basic 6 Black Book: Indispensable Problem Solver.* Albany, NY: Coriolis Technology Press, 1998.

Hunt, John. *Smalltalk and Object Orientation: An Introduction.* London: Springer-Verlag London Ltd., 1997.

Low, Graham C. and D. Ross Jeffrey. "Function Points in the Estimation and Evaluation of the Software Process", *IEEE Transactions on Software Engineering*, Vol. 16, No. 1, January 1990.

Martin, James and Carma McClure. *Structured Techniques: The Basis for CASE*, revised ed. Englewood Cliffs, NJ: Prentice Hall, 1988.

Muller, Pierre-Alain. *Instant UML.* Birmingham, U.K.: Wrox Press Ltd., 1997.

Negrino, Tom and Dori Smith. *JavaScript for the World Wide Web: Visual Quickstart Guide*, 2nd ed. Berkeley, CA: Peachpit Press, 1998.

O'Connell, Fergus. *How to Run Successful Projects II: The Silver Bullet*. New York: Prentice Hall, 1996.

Taylor, David A. *Object-Oriented Technology: A Manager's Guide*. Reading, MA: Addison-Wesley Publishing Company, 1990.

Webster, Bruce F. *Pitfalls of Object-Oriented Development*. New York: M & T Books, 1995.

INDEX